First Aid

Prevention

BABY+LIFE

BABY + LIFE

Help Your Child in a Life-Threatening Emergency. Learn What You Can Do to Prevent One from Happening.

NOEL MERENSTEIN

Illustrations by Steve Biasi

DOUBLEDAY
New York London Toronto Sydney Auckland

PUBLISHED BY DOUBLEDAY
a division of Bantam Doubleday Dell Publishing Group, Inc.
666 Fifth Avenue, New York, New York 10103

DOUBLEDAY and the portrayal of an anchor
with a dolphin are trademarks of Doubleday,
a division of Bantam Doubleday Dell
Publishing Group, Inc.

Library of Congress Cataloging-in-Publication Data
Merenstein, Noel.
    Baby-life : how to help your child in a life-threatening
emergency and what you can do to prevent one from happening /
Noel Merenstein. — 1st ed.
        p.   cm.
    1. CPR (First aid) for infants—Popular works.   2. CPR (First aid)
for children—Popular works.   3. Children's accidents—Prevention.
I. Title.
RJ370.M473   1990
618.92′1025—dc20   89-23469
                                                             CIP
    ISBN 0-385-41243-6

BOOK DESIGN BY C. MALCOLM

IMPORTANT NOTE

AUTHOR'S NOTE

To all those tiny and young souls
whose years have been cut short
and to all those who are just beginning
their journey through life . . .
May God hold them all
in His loving embrace
and keep their spirits
forever joyful and safe.

FOREWORD

Childhood safety is one of a parent's greatest concerns, and its safeguarding is one of the pediatrician's greatest responsibilities. Yet accidental injury is the leading cause of death for children in this country.

Pediatricians have an understanding of child development that makes them eminently qualified to advise parents about the safety risks a child faces at each developmental stage. Most pediatricians, however, don't have the time to provide such counseling to every family. One recent study showed that in the course of an average fifteen-minute office visit, less than one minute was devoted to a discussion of safety.

Seven years ago, this serious problem was promptly recognized and effectively handled by Noel Merenstein, who developed BABY-LIFE, a program that provides safety education to parents of young children. BABY-LIFE quickly became a New York parents' tradition and is currently being taught in several cities across the country.

Now the founder of this important educational program has written the *BABY-LIFE* book. Detailed, descriptive, and precise, this is a book that can help you save your child's life. The book includes comprehensive step-by-step instructions for administering CPR, what to do if a child is choking, how to prevent household accidents, and more. With large-sized pictorial representations of the ABC's of any conceivable life-threatening situation, the *BABY-LIFE* book leaves nothing to the reader's imagination. I found the book gripping and compelling. The writing is forceful, emphatic, and to the point. The book is anxiety-provoking and at the same time anxiety-allaying.

The author's approach is highly organized and rational. Every conceivable risk is discussed. Reading the *BABY-LIFE* book will heighten parental awareness and promote accident prevention beyond that which the pediatrician can provide. It is, therefore, one of the most meaningful contributions to preventive medicine and parental education.

JUDITH GOLDSTEIN, M.D.

ASSOCIATE DIRECTOR
DEPARTMENT OF PEDIATRICS
LENOX HILL HOSPITAL
NEW YORK, NY

CLINICAL ASSISTANT PROFESSOR
OF PEDIATRICS
NEW YORK MEDICAL COLLEGE
VALHALLA, NY

ACKNOWLEDGMENTS

There are some very special people whose help was invaluable to the *BABY-LIFE* book. They deserve praise, recognition, and my gratitude.

Roseann Hirsch helped with the writing, and her talent and experience have gone a long way in helping make this book a reality.

Steve Biasi's skill and willingness to make the illustrations as clear and accurate as possible have made this a much more useful book.

Martha Wemple was a wonderful help with editing, proofreading, and correcting the manuscript. Her keen intelligence, great enthusiasm, and attention to detail have truly helped make this a better book.

Lois Beekman offered strong support. She continually reviewed the manuscript and artwork, and offered advice that helped immeasurably.

Pam Bernstein, my agent at William Morris, was one of the first to recognize the importance of this project, and her persistence helped get it published.

Nancy Evans, President and Publisher of Doubleday, believed in the BABY-LIFE message enough to publish the book.

Judith Kern, my editor at Doubleday, has made working on this project a pleasure. Her cooperative spirit and contributions have been a real plus to the book.

Several pediatricians, particularly **Dr. Judith Goldstein** and **Dr. Richard L. Saphir,** took the time to read the *BABY-LIFE* manuscript and offered not only sound counsel, but their support as well.

Dr. David Herndon, Chief of Staff, Shriners Burns Institute, and **Dr. Barry Rumack,** Professor of Pediatrics, Director, Rocky Mountain Poison and Drug Center, also contributed their expert advice and guidance.

Cathy Berkhan was there in the early days of BABY-LIFE. I will always be thankful for her help and encouragement.

CONTENTS

Part I
Introduction

Part II
Lifesaving Information:
Opening the Airway, Breathing for Your Child, and CPR

Part III
Lifesaving Information:
Clearing an Obstructed Airway

Part IV
Additional Lifesaving Information

Part V
Prevention: Playing It Safe!

Part VI
First Aid

Part VII
Important Safety Tips

Part I
Introduction

WHAT IS BABY-LIFE?

Accidents are the leading cause of death and serious injury in infants and children.

- One child chokes to death every five days!

- Close to 600,000 pediatric burn injuries are reported annually

- Each year, over 8,000 children die as a result of accidents, and thousands more are left permanently disabled

BABY-LIFE is trying to change these statistics . . .

A mother who had taken the BABY-LIFE class had just put her nine-week-old baby daughter in her crib for the evening. A few minutes after she left the baby's room, the baby suddenly started to cry—a cry the mother had never heard before and that quickly turned into a high-pitched scream.

Despite the mother's best efforts to calm her baby, nothing worked. Then things got worse: the color drained from the baby's face, she went limp and seemed to have stopped breathing!

Panic-stricken, but realizing her baby was in a life-threatening situation, the mother grabbed the baby and dashed out of her apartment building to hail a cab to go to the nearest hospital emergency room.

While in the cab, despite her panic, she remembered what she had heard in her BABY-LIFE class: "Do something. Anything is better than nothing." The mother began to breathe for her baby—not as well as she'd learned in class, but she did remember to tilt her baby's head back so her tongue wouldn't block her airway. Rushing into the emergency room, the mother screamed, "My baby's not breathing!" A medical team took over and the baby's life was saved. Doctors later told the mother that her baby had almost died and that she had saved her baby's life.*

BABY-LIFE is a four-hour course that shows parents how to help their child in a life-threatening situation and what they can do to keep dangerous accidents from happening in the first place. It was started seven years ago, and there is no other program quite like it.

Parents are told how to handle their panic if their child is in a life-threat-

---

*This and other narratives in this book are based on real-life incidents. The names and some of the details have been changed to protect the privacy of those involved.

ening situation—you must save your child whether you panic or not. The course helps make lifesaving skills an automatic response, shows parents how to open their child's airway, how to breathe for their child, how to administer CPR, and when and how to use the Heimlich maneuver.

The course also tells parents how not to waste precious minutes when calling for help, and exactly what to say to get the fastest response. It tells parents which toys are safe—and which could be lethal—and which of their child's favorite foods could actually cause him to choke to death. Perhaps most important of all, BABY-LIFE points out the hidden child-safety hazards found in most homes and tells parents what they can do to prevent a life-threatening emergency from happening in the first place.

The BABY-LIFE class is unique because of its teaching methods. Instructors are direct and forceful. Parents listen and participate, and they learn.

Parents from all walks of life have taken BABY-LIFE classes. Lawyers, art directors, engineers, stockbrokers, secretaries, writers, and factory workers have learned lifesaving techniques from the class. So have doctors, nurses, and child-care workers. Pediatricians have

come to BABY-LIFE and then have insisted that parents take the course.

Well-known parents such as Meryl Streep, Candice Bergen, Jill Krementz and Kurt Vonnegut, Peter Jennings, Garry Trudeau, Jane Curtin, Rudolph Giuliani, Dan Greenburg, Jules Feiffer, and Lucie Arnaz have taken BABY-LIFE classes.

Church basements and Y's, synagogues, schools, and community centers are just some of the places around the country where BABY-LIFE classes have been given. They have also been given in private homes, for enthusiastic parents who have organized interested groups of their friends.

BABY-LIFE has attracted national media attention. It was featured on the popular ABC-TV program *20/20* after one of their reporters, John Stossel, took a class. BABY-LIFE has been covered on ABC's *Eyewitness News*, CBS-TV's morning and evening news programs, and other programs such as *The Regis Philbin Show*.

Over 25,000 people have taken the BABY-LIFE class, and almost everyone who has taken it has asked for a book about the program to help them remember what they have learned. Parents want a book that explains lifesaving techniques for infants and children in the same compelling way they are explained in class.

Now, with the *BABY-LIFE* book you will have all of the information given in the course: how to do CPR if your baby's heart stops; how to breathe for him when he has stopped breathing; what to do for a child who is choking; emergency first aid for bleeding, broken bones, burns, poisonings, and convulsions—techniques everyone who is around children should know something about.

The *BABY-LIFE* book also provides basic information all parents should have but often don't. For instance, it explains why you look for a baby's pulse in his arm and a child's pulse in his neck, and it points out that this is the *one* thing you can actually practice on your child *before* a life-threatening emergency happens. The book shares professional strategies used by emergency medical technicians, such as counting out loud when using lifesaving techniques to help you stay focused and to keep from becoming panic-stricken.

The accident-prevention section of the book goes beyond the traditional approach and actually awakens your own natural instincts for protecting your child. You learn how best to create a safe environment and keep your child out of harm's way.

As instructors in BABY-LIFE classes point out: "Your job as a parent is not to teach your child how to read at six months. It is to protect him and make sure he grows up safely."

Note: Please remember that as valuable as the *BABY-LIFE* book is, *IT IS NO SUBSTITUTE FOR TAKING A CPR COURSE*, given by certified instructors, where you can learn and practice life-saving techniques on mannequins. In fact, everyone in your household who cares for an infant or young child should take a CPR course. Contact your local chapter of the American Heart Association or Red Cross to find out about CPR classes or contact:

BABY-LIFE
(212-744-0805)

YOUR PRECIOUS CHILD

The BABY-LIFE book is about basic life support—the ability to keep your child alive when he can no longer keep himself alive.

There is nothing more precious to you than your child, and if he is ever in a life-threatening emergency, you will be doing something miraculous if you save his life. You will literally be giving him his whole life over again!

You will probably never be faced with the sight of your child not breathing—but it could happen. If you knew what to do, and did it quickly enough, you could save his life.

On the other hand, if you didn't know what to do, you could possibly lose your child forever . . .

A father was alone with his son. The boy was putting paper in his mouth and suddenly began to choke. He turned pale, was unable to cough, and made croaking noises when he tried to breathe. The father hit him on the back, but it didn't help. The child's lips began to turn blue. The father realized he was in trouble. At the time, he lived ten blocks from a hospital, so the father picked up his son and tried to make a run for it. The little boy choked to death in his father's arms.

A couple was at home with their nine-month-old daughter. The mother was bathing the little girl, and she did something foolish—she turned her back on her child to get a dry towel. While she wasn't watching, her baby slipped under the water. When the mother turned around, she quickly scooped her baby out of the bath. The whole incident couldn't have taken more than a minute or so, and yet the child's lips had already turned blue, and she didn't seem to be breathing! The mother turned her upside down and hit her on the back. She frantically did whatever she thought she was supposed to do, but nothing worked. Her little girl still wasn't breathing. The father called an ambulance, and they got her to the hospital. Doctors tried everything they could to revive the child, but they couldn't get her back. She was pronounced dead.

There is nothing sadder than not knowing what to do or doing the wrong thing when your child needs you most! If the father whose little boy choked to death had only known how to clear an obstructed airway, or if the mother whose little girl drowned had been able to breathe for her child when she stopped breathing, these stories might have had very different endings.

Attempting to keep somebody alive or bring somebody back to life is not a new idea. People have been doing some form of what we now call basic life support since the beginning of time. There are many references in the Bible to the "breath of life"; there is even a story where a baby who stops breathing is revived. Perhaps these are the earliest recorded examples of saving a child's life by breathing for him. Breathing is one of the first things you would most likely have to do for your baby in a life-threatening situation—*open his airway and breathe for him* if he stops breathing for himself!

Little Billy, eleven months old, was just learning to walk. He was in the backyard with his mother while she was talking to a neighbor. She turned her back for a moment, and little Billy tumbled face down into a wading pool filled with only a few inches of water. By the time his mother realized what had happened, she found Billy in the water not breathing and screamed, "My baby's dead! Somebody help me!" Her next-door neighbor, hearing the yelling, came running across the yard. He

placed little Billy on his back, tipped his head back slightly to open the airway, and started breathing for the baby. Suddenly the baby vomited water and food and began to breathe. Billy's mother thanked God for putting her neighbor in the right place at the right time.

This is a good example of spontaneous resuscitation. One minute your child is not breathing; you open his airway and breathe for him, and he begins breathing on his own spontaneously.

Sometimes, however, it takes longer for a child to come back, and you may also have to do more than just breathe for him . . .

"I was only away a few minutes," said one mother, who only went to answer the phone. She didn't leave her child alone for an hour, but only for a few minutes.

While the mother was gone, her older daughter, Sarah, three, left the back door open and little fifteen-month-old Lisa crawled out and fell into the backyard pool. By the time Lisa's mother got off the phone and went out to the yard, she found her daughter floating, lifeless, in the pool. She screamed for her husband, who, fortunately, was trained in CPR. He quickly determined that Lisa had not only stopped breathing, but her little heart had stopped as well. He immediately began doing a combination of breathing into the baby and pumping for her heart—cardiopulmonary resuscitation.

In this case, however, the baby did not "come back" right away. It wasn't until they got her to the hospital, and after a lot of hard work by the doctors and prayer by the parents, that Lisa began breathing on her own.

Unlike little Billy, who came back spontaneously, Lisa took longer to begin functioning fully on her own. This is why it is so important *not to give up* when you are doing any lifesaving effort, even if the child doesn't respond immediately. You must keep up your lifesaving efforts until medical help arrives and takes over!

HOW TO USE THE BABY-LIFE BOOK

If your child is ever involved in a life-threatening emergency, you'll have to be prepared to act immediately. There won't be enough time to learn what to do to save his life at that moment. So read this book *now*, from beginning to end, and then go back and reread a little each day to make sure you fully understand the lifesaving techniques described.

Remember: No matter how many times you read this, or any other book, it is not a substitute for the hands-on mannequin practice you get when taking a CPR course!

The lifesaving information in the book is repeated in separate sections entitled "Infant/Baby" (newborn to one year of age) and "Child" (from one to eight years of age). This is because when doing CPR, breathing for your child, or clearing an obstructed airway, the techniques you need to use change when your child is a year old. However, the changes are actually based more on your child's size than his age: For instance, if your thirteen-month-old child is very small, you might still be able to use some of the lifesaving techniques for infants. On the other hand, if your baby is very large by eleven months, you may have to use some of the techniques for an older child.

The information in this book is repeated often to help you remember it. In fact, instructors use repetition when they are teaching BABY-LIFE classes because it is a particularly effective way to make sure that parents don't forget what they have learned.

After you have read the lifesaving information, study the drawings that accompany it. There are illustrations that give you an overall view as well as detailed close-ups of each lifesaving technique. The "Common Mistakes" section of the book points out some of the most frequent—and dangerous—mistakes made by parents taking the BABY-LIFE class when practicing breathing and CPR on the mannequins. The "Questions and Answers" section deals with the questions most often asked by parents in the classes, and may answer some of your own questions about lifesaving.

You may want to read the "Prevention" section first, since this will explain what you can do *now* to prevent a life-threatening emergency from happening in the first place.

Read the "First Aid" section of the book to familiarize yourself with the general first-aid procedures you might need for bleeding, poisoning, burns, or other serious emergencies. You can follow up by taking a first-aid course to learn more.

Note: The information in the *BABY-LIFE* book is based on the most recent medical standards and guidelines. However, lifesaving and first-aid techniques are continually changing and improving, and it is your responsibility to stay up to date on the latest techniques. Take CPR and first-aid courses regularly to stay current.

Part II
Lifesaving Information: Opening the Airway, Breathing for Your Child, and CPR

THE BASICS OF STAYING ALIVE

In a life-threatening situation, especially if *your* child is involved, you will have difficulty remembering your own name, let alone complicated lifesaving instructions.

What you do need to know is: *Your child needs oxygen to stay alive.* Every cell in his body needs a constant supply of oxygen. His brain cells, the most sensitive cells of all, need it continuously and without interruption. What you also need to know is that your child gets his oxygen from the air he breathes.

When he is healthy and every system in his body is functioning properly, your child is supplied with oxygen by breathing through his *AIRWAY*. The airway is his body's most important passageway. His nose, mouth, throat, and windpipe make up your child's airway, and there is no other way for precious oxygen to get into his little body.

Your child gets the oxygen he needs by *BREATHING*. Take a deep breath—inhale, exhale—that's breathing! Your child does it automatically every moment of his life.

Once your child has taken in the oxygen he needs to live—through his *airway* by *breathing*—the oxygen he has just inhaled into his lungs must pass quickly to every cell in his body (especially his brain cells). Here is where *CIRCULATION* takes over.

Your child's heart pumps his blood. The blood picks up the oxygen from his lungs, and the oxygen-rich blood is circulated throughout his body. Every cell is bathed continually with this life-giving oxygen. Circulation is an ongoing process that is never interrupted.

AIRWAY, BREATHING, CIRCULATION: Say these words out loud now several times. Learn them! They are the ABC's—the *basics of staying alive*. They are also the basics of lifesaving and will help guide you if your child is in an emergency.

Anything that blocks your child's airway, interferes with his breathing, or stops his circulation puts him in a life-threatening situation. For infants and children, most life-threatening situations usually involve breathing—the child either stops breathing or has great difficulty breathing. This can be caused by choking, suffocation, strangulation, drowning, smoke inhalation, or illness. Sometimes an infant will simply stop breathing for no apparent reason, as in sudden infant death syndrome.

But even after breathing has stopped, a child's heart can actually go on beating. The heart will soon give out, however, and when there is no heartbeat (no pulse) and no breathing, the baby is *clinically dead.*

Within four to six minutes after clinical death, irreversible damage to the brain begins. The brain cells start to die because of a lack of oxygen.

This means that you might have only a few minutes to save your child's life. *YOU MUST TRY TO GET EMERGENCY MEDICAL HELP AS QUICKLY AS POSSIBLE.*

However, since the average response time for many ambulances is at least eight to twelve minutes, you must *also* take immediate steps *yourself* to help save your child's life. Remembering *AIRWAY, BREATHING, CIRCULATION* reminds you what to do first for your child until help arrives.

INFANT/BABY
(NEWBORN TO ONE YEAR)

STEP ONE: OPEN YOUR BABY'S AIRWAY

If your baby is ever involved in a life-threatening situation, you may see it happen . . .

Your curious baby is crawling on the living-room floor when he suddenly unplugs an extension cord and puts the live end in his mouth. Or he grabs your house keys and puts one of them into an electrical outlet.

Or you may see nothing at all . . .

You put the baby down in his crib for the evening. He seems fine. A half hour later you decide to check on him, but now the baby doesn't look right. His color is off. He is lying very still. Something is wrong.

Whether you see something happen or not, once you discover your baby needs help, you must take action! The first thing you must do is try to wake your baby and get him to respond by stimulating him. You can do this in two ways:

1. *USE YOUR VOICE:* Call out, "Baby, baby, are you all right?" If he is only sleeping, just the sound of your voice is often enough to get him to respond.

2. *USE GENTLE PHYSICAL STIMULATION:* Flick the bottom of the baby's feet. Gently pat and nudge the baby, or even pinch his skin to arouse him.

Does the baby move? Does he open his eyes? Does he make any noises? If your baby does not move, make a noise, or has not responded to any stimulation, he is unconscious and in a life-threatening emergency!

You don't know what is wrong with your baby, but you do know it is serious.

Your first instinct will be to run to the phone for help. That's a good instinct—you need to get emergency medical help as quickly as possible. So *YELL FOR HELP!* Yell as loudly as you can! If someone is nearby, tell him to call **911** or your local Emergency Medical Services (EMS) number. But you must not leave the baby yet. *You have to take some immediate steps to save your baby's life.* You have to remember *AIRWAY, BREATHING, CIRCULATION.*

The first thing you must do is *OPEN YOUR BABY'S AIRWAY:*

1. Place your baby on his back, on a firm surface. If you have to move him to do this, carefully support his head, neck, and body and turn him as a unit. This is especially important if your baby has taken a bad fall, or if you suspect a neck or spine injury.*

2. With your baby lying flat, open his airway by putting one or two fingers under the bony part of his chin (do not press on the soft tissue of the neck, which could close off his airway). Lift the chin gently. Make sure your baby's mouth remains partially open when lifting the chin. At the same time, put your other hand on the baby's forehead and tilt his head back *slightly.* *CAREFUL!* Don't tilt his head back

too far, as this may actually close off his airway. Tilt it back into a level position, as if the baby were looking straight up at the ceiling.

When a baby (or anyone) is unconscious, the muscles of the throat become so relaxed that the tongue rests on the back of the throat, blocks the air passage, and prevents the baby from breathing. When you lift the chin and tilt the head back slightly, the tongue comes forward off the baby's throat and his air passage is cleared. Sometimes just doing this vital step— opening the airway—will allow your baby to start breathing and save his life!

* **Caution:** Never move a baby if you suspect a neck or spine injury, unless it is absolutely necessary to move him to save his life.

If you have to move your baby, and you do suspect he has a neck or spine injury from a bad fall, head injury, or car accident, for instance):
1. Move him as a unit, supporting his head, neck, and body as carefully as possible, so that his head does not roll, turn, or twist in any direction. Keep his head, neck, shoulders, back, and legs in a straight line.
2. Open his airway by carefully lifting or pulling his jaw forward *without* tilting his head back. To learn this technique correctly, take a CPR course.

OPENING THE AIRWAY

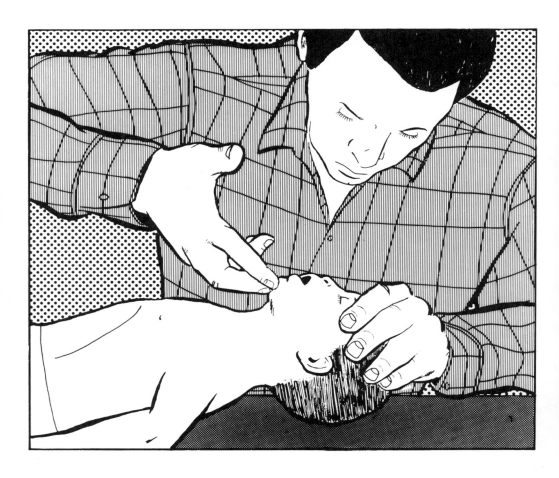

TRY TO WAKE YOUR BABY

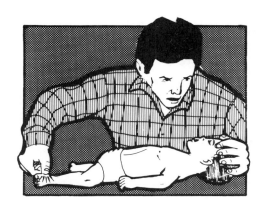

1. Use your voice. Call out, "Baby, baby, are you all right?"

2. Use physical stimulation. Flick the bottom of your baby's feet. Gently pat and nudge him, or even pinch his skin to arouse him.

LIFT YOUR BABY'S CHIN

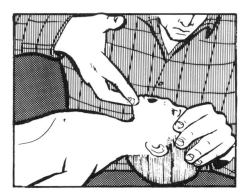

With your baby lying flat, put one or two fingers under the bony part of his chin (do not press on the soft tissue of his neck). Lift his chin gently. Make sure your baby's mouth remains partially open when lifting his chin.

TILT YOUR BABY'S HEAD BACK SLIGHTLY

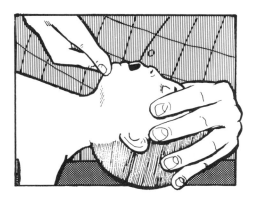

At the same time, put your other hand on your baby's forehead and tilt his head back *slightly*. Don't tilt his head back too far, as this may actually close off his airway.

STEP TWO: CHECK FOR BREATHING — GIVE TWO BREATHS

Opening the airway is the first step in saving your baby's life. Now you must *check to see if he is breathing.* (This is probably something you've done almost every night since he was born!):

1. *Watch your baby's chest and stomach.* Is there any movement? Is his chest rising and falling?

2. *Put your face near your baby's nose and mouth.* Feel for his breath on your cheek.

3. *Put your ear close to your baby's nose and mouth.* Do you hear any sounds of breathing?

If you see nothing, feel nothing, and hear nothing, your baby is not breathing! When this happens, there is only one way to save his life: *You must get air into him immediately!*

GIVE YOUR BABY TWO BREATHS:

1. While keeping your baby's airway open, cover his nose and mouth with your mouth and make an airtight seal. Blow a *slow* breath into him. Blow into your baby only long enough and with just enough force to make his chest rise. *YOU MUST SEE YOUR BABY'S CHEST RISE WHEN YOU BLOW A BREATH INTO HIM.* Then take your mouth off your baby's mouth and nose to let the air out of him. Take another breath yourself.

2. Once again make an airtight seal over your baby's nose and mouth with your mouth. Blow another slow breath into your baby only long enough and with just enough force to make his chest rise.

Note: If you can't make the chest rise when you blow a breath into your baby, you may have tilted his head back too far, or you may not have tilted it back far enough and his tongue may still be blocking his airway. *Try opening the* *airway again.* Lift his chin, reposition the head by tilting it back slightly, and try a second time to blow a slow breath into him. If you still can't get the chest to rise, the airway may be blocked by food, a toy, or some other foreign object, and you will have to try to clear the obstruction. (See Part III, "Clearing an Obstructed Airway," page 69.)

Caution: Breathing too forcefully could cause air to inflate your baby's stomach, which could prevent air from getting into the lungs, or cause vomiting. Vomiting is one of the biggest hazards to a baby. Whatever he has thrown up could go into his lungs.

If your baby has already vomited when you find him, *or if you see any other foreign matter in his mouth,* or if he vomits while you are doing a life-saving procedure, you must turn him on his side immediately and clean out his mouth to keep his airway and lungs clear.

Parents taking the BABY-LIFE course frequently express concern that they are breathing carbon dioxide into the baby's lungs while they are breathing for him. However, since the air you inhale contains 21 percent oxygen, and the air you exhale contains as much as 16 percent oxygen, your baby is still getting a considerable amount of life-giving oxygen.

CHECKING FOR BREATHING

WATCH YOUR BABY'S CHEST AND STOMACH

Is there any movement? Is his chest rising and falling?

PUT YOUR FACE NEAR YOUR BABY'S NOSE AND MOUTH

Feel for his breath on your cheek.

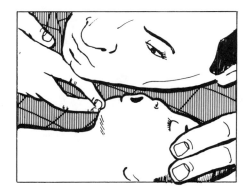

PUT YOUR EAR CLOSE TO YOUR BABY'S NOSE AND MOUTH

Do you hear any sounds of breathing?

GIVING THE FIRST TWO BREATHS

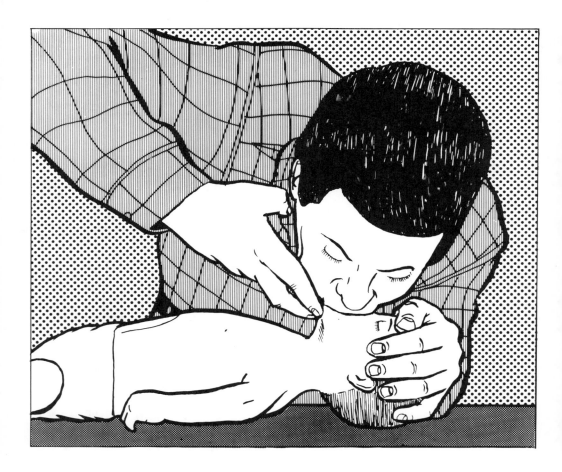

MAKE AN AIRTIGHT SEAL

Cover your baby's nose and mouth with your mouth, and make an air-tight seal.

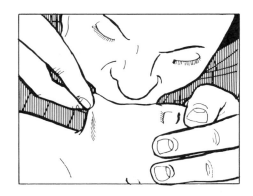

BLOW A SLOW BREATH INTO YOUR BABY

With your baby's airway open, blow a *slow* breath into him. Blow only long enough and with just enough force to make his chest rise. Look out of the corner of your eye as you blow a breath in, to make sure your baby's chest rises.

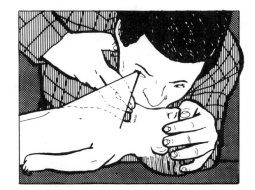

TAKE YOUR MOUTH OFF YOUR BABY

As soon as his chest rises, take your mouth off your baby's mouth to let the air out, and to take another breath yourself. Make an airtight seal again, and give your baby a second breath.

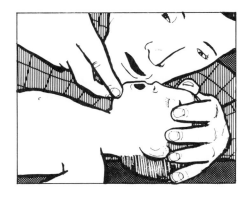

STEP THREE: CHECK FOR CIRCULATION— DOES YOUR BABY HAVE A PULSE?

You have now opened your baby's airway by lifting his chin and tilting his head back slightly. You have also breathed two slow breaths into him, getting oxygen into his lungs, and you have seen his chest rise with each breath.

Once you have breathed air into your baby's lungs, you must determine whether the oxygen-rich blood is being circulated around the body. Your baby's brain is the most sensitive part of his body and needs oxygen most continuously and without interruption.

The only way to find out whether oxygen is being circulated throughout the body is to find your baby's pulse. The pulse is a reflection of the heartbeat. If there is a pulse, you know that your baby's heart is beating, and the oxygen-rich blood is being circulated around the body and is getting to the brain and all the other vital organs.

FIND YOUR BABY'S PULSE IN THE UPPER ARM. (This is called the brachial pulse.):

1. Using your first two or three fingers (not your thumb—it has a pulse of its own and could mislead you), gently press the inside of the upper arm between the elbow and the armpit. You may not find the pulse the first place you press, and you'll have to search for it by moving your fingers up or down and pressing again. Check both arms—if you don't feel the pulse in one arm, try the other. Because it is difficult to find a baby's brachial pulse, be sure to give yourself up to ten seconds to locate it. While you are finding your baby's pulse, remember to keep his head tilted back slightly so that his airway remains open.

2. If you find your baby's pulse, go back and check his breathing again. Since he has a pulse, this means his heart is beating and his blood is circulating. But he still may not be breathing on his own. If this is the case, *you must continue to breathe for him!*

Note: If your baby has *no pulse,* you must begin CPR immediately! (See Part II, "CPR! Breathing for Your Baby and Doing Chest Compressions," page 32.)

Learning to find your baby's pulse is the only thing *you as a parent can practice on your baby* before *a life-threatening emergency happens.* **Never practice any lifesaving technique in this book on any living thing.** *At BABY-LIFE the importance of parents' knowing how to take their baby's pulse is continually stressed. If you have trouble locating your baby's pulse when you practice, ask your pediatrician to help you.*

FINDING THE PULSE

USE YOUR FIRST TWO OR THREE FINGERS

Find your baby's pulse with your first two or three fingers. Don't use your thumb—it has a pulse of its own.

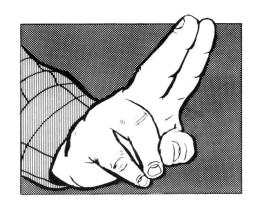

FIND YOUR BABY'S BRACHIAL PULSE

Your baby's brachial pulse is located on the inside of his upper arm, between his elbow and his armpit.

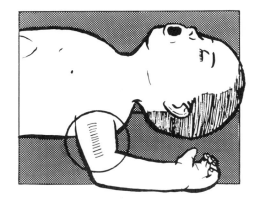

GENTLY PRESS THE INSIDE OF THE UPPER ARM

If you don't feel the pulse, move your fingers up or down the arm and press again, or try the other arm. Give yourself up to ten seconds to locate the pulse. (If baby has a pulse, see p. 28. If baby has no pulse, see p. 32.)

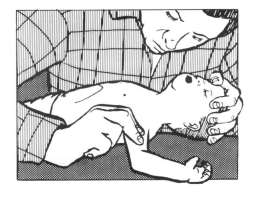

BREATHING FOR YOUR BABY

"THE BREATH OF LIFE"

If your baby has a pulse, but does not start breathing on his own after you give him the first two breaths, *you must begin breathing for your baby regularly to keep him supplied with oxygen.*

BREATHE FOR YOUR BABY (at approximately the same rate he would breathe if he were able to do it on his own):

1. While keeping the airway open by lifting the chin and tilting the head back slightly, cover your baby's nose and mouth with your mouth, making an airtight seal. Blow a *slow* breath into your baby. Blow only long enough and with just enough force to make his chest rise. *Remember to look out of the corner of your eye each time you blow a breath into him to see his chest rise.* Then take your mouth off the baby to let the air out of him.

2. Once again make an airtight seal with your mouth over the baby's nose and mouth. Blow another slow breath into the baby, again only long enough and with just enough force to make his chest rise. Remember to take your mouth off your baby after each breath in order to let the air out of him and take a breath yourself.

3. Breathe into your baby as regularly as you can—one breath every three seconds (at least twenty breaths per minute). Count out loud: "One thousand one, one thousand two"—*breathe!* Counting out loud keeps you focused and can help control panic. It forces you to concentrate and to breathe normally, and can prevent you from hyperventilating. Keep in mind that you are actually breathing for your baby! If you stop, he will have no air.

4. After one minute (about twenty breaths), stop and check your baby's pulse and breathing. Use your first two or three fingers (not your thumb) and gently press the inside of your baby's upper arm, between the elbow and the armpit. If his

pulse is still there, check for breathing. If he has not yet started to breathe on his own, keep breathing for him until he breathes on his own, or until emergency medical help arrives!

Note: *If, after one minute* of breathing for your baby, no one has answered your cries for help, come to your aid, or summoned emergency medical help, you must continue your lifesaving efforts, but now *YOU MUST GET HELP* yourself by calling **911** or your local Emergency Medical Services number. While you are waiting for help to arrive, *continue breathing for your baby.* Every minute or so, check for your baby's pulse and to see if he has started breathing on his own. If your baby does start breathing on his own but remains unconscious, you must *still keep his airway open* and continue to watch him closely to make sure he keeps breathing and has a pulse. (See Part IV, "How to Get Emergency Medical Help!" page 106.)

BREATHING FOR YOUR BABY

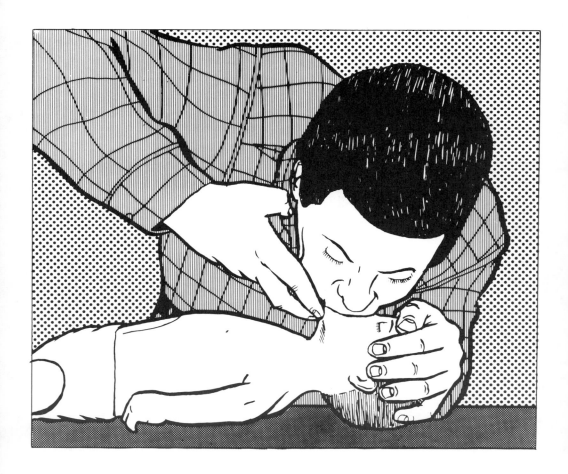

BLOW A SLOW BREATH INTO YOUR BABY

Cover your baby's nose and mouth with your mouth, and make an airtight seal. Blow a *slow* breath into him, just enough to make his chest rise. Look out of the corner of your eye as you blow a breath in, to be sure your baby's chest rises.

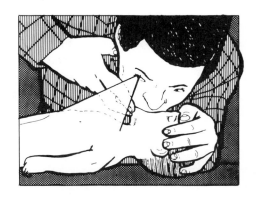

TAKE YOUR MOUTH OFF YOUR BABY

Take your mouth off the baby's mouth and nose to let the air out of him and to take another breath yourself.

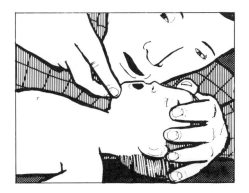

BLOW ANOTHER SLOW BREATH INTO YOUR BABY

Continue to breathe into your baby— one breath every three seconds—taking your mouth off your baby between breaths to let the air out of him and to take another breath yourself.

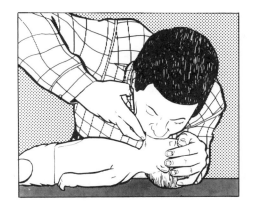

CPR! BREATHING FOR YOUR BABY AND DOING CHEST COMPRESSIONS

NO PULSE! If your baby has no pulse, that means his heart has stopped beating and there is no circulation. *YOU MUST BEGIN CPR IMMEDIATELY!*

You must do the work of the heart and the lungs by performing CPR—cardiopulmonary resuscitation. Now you will not only breathe for your baby, you will do the pumping for his heart as well.

YOU DO CPR FOR ONE REASON ONLY—NO PULSE—and you are the one who will have to determine if your baby has no pulse, and whether you must do CPR. To avoid doing CPR unnecessarily, learn how to find your baby's pulse and practice finding it *before* an emergency happens!

CPR HAS RISKS! Even doing it correctly, you could do damage to your baby. If you do it wrong, you can do irreversible damage! However, if your baby has stopped breathing, and you cannot find his pulse, then *CPR COULD*

SAVE HIS LIFE! But you must do it right.

When you do CPR, you will be pressing on your baby's sternum. (The sternum is the breastbone, which runs down the center of the chest.) You must press *exactly* in the right place. If you push too low on the sternum you can cause a serious, even fatal injury. At the bottom tip of the sternum is a fragile piece of cartilage called the *xiphoid process*. If pressed, this triangular-shaped cartilage could scrape or lacerate the liver and cause severe internal bleeding. On either side of the sternum are the ribs. If you press directly on the baby's ribs, you could easily break or splinter a rib, which could puncture a lung or other vital organ. Pressing too high on the sternum or using jabbing or poking motions to compress the sternum could also be dangerous, and you might not be effective in circulating the blood carrying precious oxygen to the brain.

Don't forget, if the brain isn't supplied with oxygen, irreversible damage will occur after four to six minutes. So if CPR is *delayed*, or if you do CPR *improperly*, even if your baby is revived he could still be seriously impaired.

This is why you *must* be properly trained to do CPR in a course given by

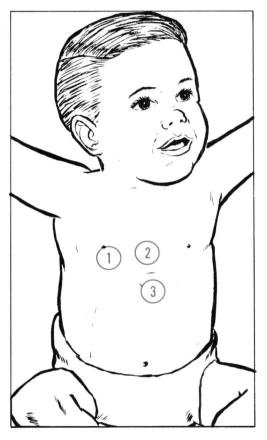 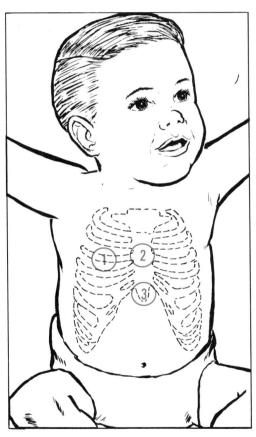

(1) BABY'S RIB CAGE (DO NOT PRESS)
(2) STERNUM
(3) XIPHOID PROCESS (DO NOT PRESS)

certified instructors, where you will learn the correct techniques by practicing on mannequins. Practice CPR only on dolls or mannequins, *never* on any living thing!

Remember the steps before starting CPR: Carefully supporting the baby's head, neck, and body, place him on his back. Open the airway by lifting the chin and tilting the head back slightly (this moves the tongue off the windpipe). Check to see whether your baby is breathing. If he is not, blow two slow breaths into him, making the chest rise each time and removing your mouth between breaths. Then feel for his pulse for up to ten seconds. Use your first two or three fingers—not your thumb—and gently press the inside of the baby's upper arm, between the elbow and the armpit.

IF YOU FIND NO PULSE AFTER TEN SECONDS, BEGIN CPR:

1. Make sure the baby is on a firm, flat surface such as a table or the floor. (You cannot do CPR effectively on a soft surface such as a bed or a sofa.)

2. You can provide extra support for a small infant's upper back with your hand. Slip the hand closest to the baby's head under his upper back. Be careful to support his neck and let his head tilt back only *slightly* to keep his airway open. Remember not to tilt the head back too far.

3. While supporting the baby's back with the hand closest to the head, use your other hand to locate the correct place on the sternum to do CPR compressions. Draw an imaginary line with your index finger (your pointer finger) from one nipple to the other.

4. Place your index finger on the sternum just below the center of the imaginary line.

5. Put your middle finger and ring finger on the sternum below your index finger. Now, lift up your index finger. Your middle and ring fingers are now in the correct place on the sternum, one finger's width below the nipple line. (See illustration for the correct placement of your fingers.) *BE SURE YOUR FINGERS ARE NOT TOUCHING THE XIPHOID PROCESS!**

---

* **Caution:** All babies are built differently, and the sizes of parents' hands vary. If, after you have placed your fingers on the sternum (one finger's width below the nipple line), you are in danger of pressing on the xiphoid process, move your fingers slightly higher up on the sternum.

6. Using two fingers (or three if needed for a bigger baby), press the sternum straight down, one half inch to one inch, and then *release all the way*, leaving your fingers still resting lightly in place on the sternum. Continue to press and release at a *rapid rate*, being careful not to lift your fingers off the sternum between compressions. Do five compressions. Count out loud: "One, two, three, four, five." You will be doing slightly more than one compression per second.

7. After five compressions, stop pumping long enough to make an airtight seal over the baby's nose and mouth with your mouth and blow a slow breath into the baby. *Blow into your baby only long enough and with just enough force to make his chest rise.*

8. Take your mouth off the baby and give him five more compressions. Each compression should be done smoothly. Spend equal time compressing and releasing. *Do not poke or jab your baby. Never press on the xiphoid process.* Remember to press straight down (not on an angle), one half inch to one inch on each compression, and release all

the way, still leaving your fingers resting lightly on the sternum.

9. After every five compressions, blow a slow breath into the baby, just enough to make his chest rise.

Continue using the ratio of five compressions to one breath for your baby for one minute. Then stop. Try to find his pulse and check for his breathing. If you find no pulse or breathing, continue CPR. *CHECK FOR THE PULSE AND THE BREATHING EVERY MINUTE OR SO!* If you find the pulse, stop chest compressions. But if your baby has not yet started to breathe on his own, *you must keep breathing for him* (one breath every three seconds). If your baby starts breathing on his own but remains unconscious, *be sure to keep his airway open* and continue to check his pulse and breathing until help arrives.

Remember: Whether you are only breathing for your baby or doing both breathing and chest compressions, *if no one has come to your aid after one minute, continue your lifesaving efforts and GET HELP!* Call **911** or your local Emergency Medical Services number. (See Part IV, "How to Get Emergency Medical Help!" page 106).

GETTING READY TO DO CHEST COMPRESSIONS

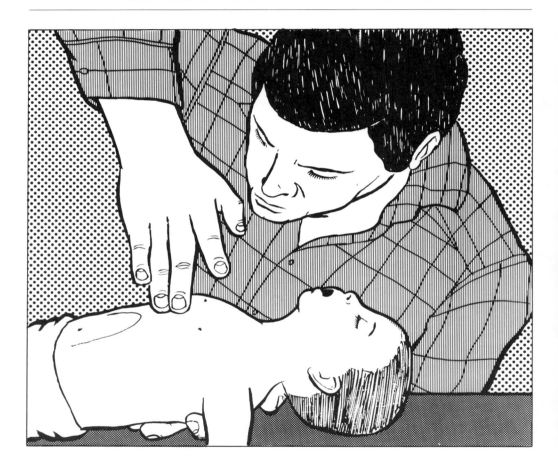

USE YOUR INDEX FINGER TO FIND THE EXACT PLACE ON THE STERNUM

Draw an imaginary line between the nipples with your index finger. Then place your index finger on the sternum, just below the center of the imaginary line.

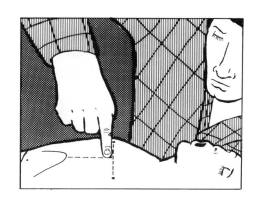

PLACE YOUR MIDDLE AND RING FINGERS ON THE STERNUM BELOW THE INDEX FINGER

Place your fingers on the sternum only. Make sure your fingers do not touch the ribs.

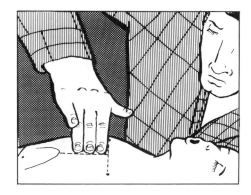

LIFT UP YOUR INDEX FINGER

Your middle and ring fingers are now in the correct position on the sternum to do the chest compressions—*one finger's width below the nipple line.* Make sure your fingers are not touching the xiphoid process.

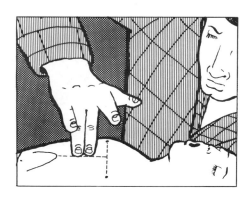

DOING CHEST COMPRESSIONS AND BREATHING FOR YOUR BABY

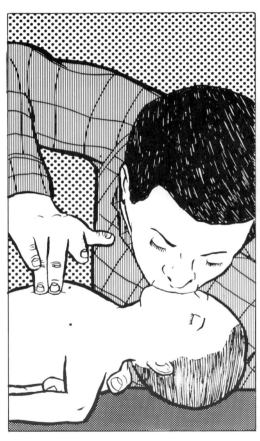

PRESS THE STERNUM STRAIGHT DOWN

Use two fingers, or three if needed for a bigger baby. Press the sternum straight down, one-half inch to one inch. (Do not press on the xiphoid process.)

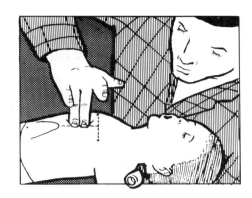

RELEASE ALL THE WAY

Release the sternum completely, leaving your fingers resting lightly in place. Press and release the sternum again. Do a total of five compressions at a rapid rate.

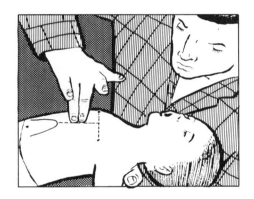

BLOW A SLOW BREATH INTO YOUR BABY

After five compressions, stop long enough to make an airtight seal with your mouth over the baby's nose and mouth. Blow a slow breath into your baby, just enough to make his chest rise. Keep repeating five chest compressions, *and* give a slow breath after every fifth compression.

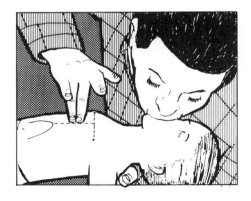

CHILD
(ONE YEAR TO EIGHT YEARS)

STEP ONE: OPEN YOUR CHILD'S AIRWAY

If your child is ever involved in a life-threatening situation, you may see it happen . . .

You are sitting by the swimming pool, chatting with a friend and watching your little girl play in the pool—but not really paying attention! Suddenly she slips out of her swim ring and disappears under the water. You jump in immediately and pull her out. She is limp and lifeless as you lay her beside the pool.

Or you may see nothing at all . . .

Your toddler is in his room. You can hear him playing with his toys. A few minutes later things seem very quiet, and you decide to check on him. You find him lying on the floor and his color is off. He is very still. Something is wrong.

Whether you see something happen or not, once you discover your child needs help, you must take action! The first thing you must do is try to wake your child and get him to respond by stimulating him. You can do this in two ways:

1. *USE YOUR VOICE:* Call out, "Child, child, are you all right?" If he is only sleeping, just the sound of your voice is often enough to get him to respond.

2. *USE GENTLE PHYSICAL STIMU-LATION:* Gently pat and nudge him, or even pinch his skin to arouse him.

Does your child move? Does he open his eyes? Does he make any noises? If your child does not move, make a noise, or has not responded to any stimulation, he is *unconscious* and in a life-threatening emergency! You don't know what is wrong with your child, but you do know it is serious!

Your first instinct will be to run to the phone for help. That's a good instinct—you need to get emergency medical help as quickly as possible. So, *YELL FOR HELP!* Yell as loudly as you can! If someone is nearby, tell them to call **911** or your local Emergency Medical Services (EMS) number. But you must not leave the child yet. *You have to take some immediate steps to save your child's life!* You have to remember *AIRWAY, BREATHING, CIRCULATION.*

The first thing you must do is *OPEN YOUR CHILD'S AIRWAY:*

1. Place your child on his back, on a firm surface. If you have to move him to do this, carefully support his head, neck, and body, and turn him as a unit. This is especially important if your child has taken a bad fall, or if you suspect a neck or spine injury.*

2. With your child lying flat, open his airway by putting one or two fingers under the bony part of his chin (do not press on the soft tissue of the neck, which could close off his airway). Lift the chin gently. Make sure your child's mouth remains partially open when lifting the chin. At the same time, put your

other hand on your child's forehead and tilt his head back *slightly.* You may have to tilt it slightly farther back than you would for an infant.

When a child (or anyone) is unconscious, the muscles of the throat can become so relaxed that the tongue rests on the back of the throat, blocks the air passage, and prevents the child from breathing. When you lift the chin and tilt the head back slightly, the tongue comes forward off the child's throat and his air passage is cleared. Sometimes just doing this vital step— opening the airway—will allow your child to start breathing and save his life.

---

* **Caution:** Never move a child if you suspect a neck or spine injury, unless it is absolutely necessary to move him to save his life.

If you have to move your child, and do suspect a neck or spine injury (from a bad fall, head injury, car accident, or diving mishap, for instance):
1. Move him as a unit, supporting his head, neck, and body as carefully as possible so that his head does not roll, turn, or twist in any direction. Keep his head, neck, shoulders, back, and legs in a straight line.
2. Open his airway by carefully lifting or pulling his jaw forward *without* tilting his head back. To learn this technique correctly, take a CPR course.

OPENING THE AIRWAY

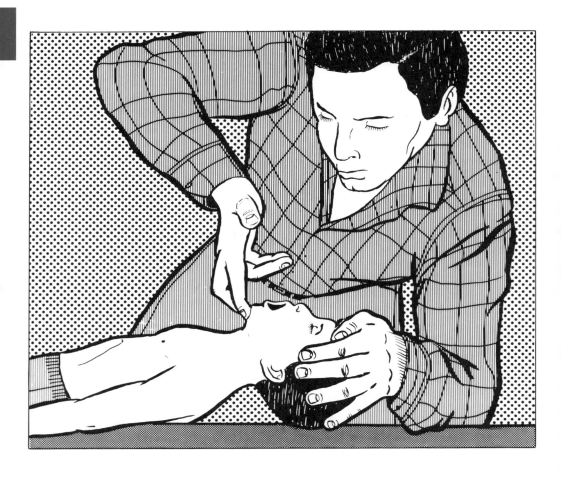

TRY TO WAKE YOUR CHILD

1. Use your voice. Call out, "Child, child, are you all right?"

2. Use physical stimulation. Gently pat and nudge him, or even pinch his skin to arouse him.

LIFT YOUR CHILD'S CHIN

With your child lying flat, put one or two fingers under the bony part of his chin (do not press on the soft tissue of his neck). Lift his chin gently. Make sure your child's mouth remains partially open when lifting the chin.

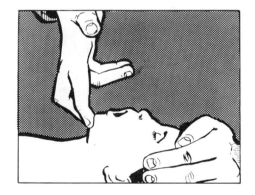

TILT YOUR CHILD'S HEAD BACK SLIGHTLY

At the same time, put your other hand on your child's forehead and tilt his head back *slightly*. You may have to tilt it slightly farther back than you would for an infant.

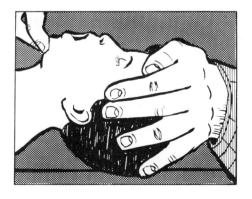

STEP TWO: CHECK FOR BREATHING— GIVE TWO BREATHS

Opening the airway is only the first step in saving your child's life. Now you must *check to see if he is breathing:*

1. *Watch your child's chest and stomach.* Is there any movement? Is his chest rising and falling?

2. *Put your face near your child's nose and mouth.* Feel for his breath on your cheek.

3. *Put your ear close to your child's nose and mouth.* Do you hear any sounds of breathing?

If you see nothing, feel nothing, and hear nothing, your child is not breathing! When this happens, there is only one way to save his life: You must get air into him immediately!

GIVE YOUR CHILD TWO BREATHS:

1. While keeping your child's airway open, pinch his nose with your thumb and index finger.* (Use the hand that is on the child's forehead to pinch his nose, remembering to keep his head tilted back slightly.) At the same time, cover your child's mouth with your mouth, making an airtight seal, and blow a *slow* breath into him. Blow into your child only long enough and with just enough force to make his chest rise. *YOU MUST SEE YOUR CHILD'S CHEST RISE WHEN YOU BLOW A BREATH INTO HIM.* Then take your mouth off your child's mouth and release his nose to let the air out of him. Take another breath yourself.

2. Once again pinch your child's nose and cover your child's mouth with your mouth, making an airtight seal, and blow another slow breath into your child, only long enough and with just enough force to make his chest rise.

---

* When you are breathing air into an infant, it is unnecessary to pinch his nose since you will be covering both his nose and mouth with your mouth. *With a child, however, it is necessary to pinch his nose* since his face is larger and you will be unable to cover both his nose and mouth with your mouth. If you blow air into your child's mouth without pinching the nose, some of the air will escape through his nose.

Note: If you can't make the chest rise when you blow a breath into your child, you may have tilted his head back too far, or you may not have tilted it back far enough and his tongue may still be blocking his airway. *Try opening the airway again.* Lift his chin, reposition the head by tilting it back slightly, and try a second time to blow a slow breath into him. If you still can't get the chest to rise, the airway may be blocked by food, a toy, or some other foreign object, and you will have to try to clear the obstruction. (See Part III, "Clearing an Obstructed Airway," page 69.)

Caution: Breathing too forcefully could cause air to inflate your child's stomach, which could prevent air from getting into the lungs, or cause vomiting. *Vomiting is one of the biggest hazards to an unconscious child. Whatever he* has thrown up can go into his lungs.

If your child has already vomited when you find him, *or if you see any other foreign matter in his mouth,* or if he vomits while you are doing a life-saving procedure, you must turn him on his side immediately and clean out his mouth to keep his airway and lungs clear.

Parents taking the BABY-LIFE course frequently express concern that they are breathing carbon dioxide into their child's lungs while they are breathing for him. However, since the air you inhale contains 21 percent oxygen, and the air you exhale contains as much as 16 percent oxygen, your child is still getting a considerable amount of life-giving oxygen.

CHECKING FOR BREATHING

WATCH YOUR CHILD'S CHEST AND STOMACH

Is there any movement? Is his chest rising and falling?

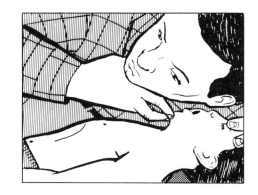

PUT YOUR FACE NEAR YOUR CHILD'S NOSE AND MOUTH

Feel for his breath on your cheek.

PUT YOUR EAR CLOSE TO YOUR CHILD'S NOSE AND MOUTH

Do you hear any sounds of breathing?

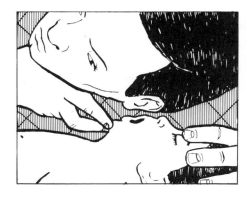

GIVING THE FIRST TWO BREATHS

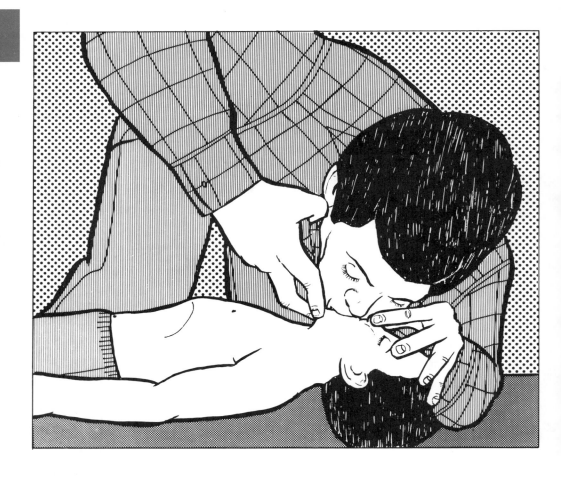

MAKE AN AIRTIGHT SEAL

Pinch your child's nose with your thumb and index finger. At the same time, cover his mouth with your mouth, making an airtight seal.

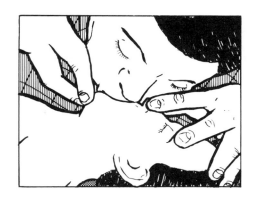

BLOW A SLOW BREATH INTO YOUR CHILD

With your child's airway open, blow a *slow* breath into him. Blow only long enough and with just enough force to make his chest rise. Look out of the corner of your eye as you blow a breath in, to make sure your child's chest rises.

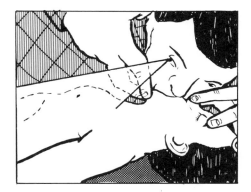

TAKE YOUR MOUTH OFF YOUR CHILD

As soon as his chest rises, take your mouth off your child's mouth (and release the nose) to let the air out, and to take another breath yourself. Pinch his nose, make an airtight seal again, and give your child a second breath.

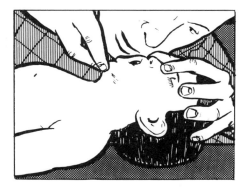

STEP THREE: CHECK FOR CIRCULATION —DOES YOUR CHILD HAVE A PULSE?

You have now opened your child's airway by lifting his chin and tilting his head back slightly. You have also breathed two slow breaths into him, getting oxygen into his lungs, and you have seen his chest rise with each breath.

Once you have breathed air into your child's lungs, you must determine whether the oxygen-rich blood is being circulated around the body. Your child's brain is the most sensitive part of his body and needs oxygen most continuously and without interruption.

The only way to find out whether oxygen is being circulated throughout the body is to find your child's pulse. The pulse is a reflection of the heartbeat. If there is a pulse, you know that your child's heart is beating, and the oxygen-rich blood is being circulated around

the body and is getting to the brain and all the other vital organs.

Now that your child is older and has lost the baby fat under his neck, you will be using the carotid pulse because it is easier to find than the brachial pulse used for infants.

FIND YOUR CHILD'S PULSE IN THE NECK. (The carotid pulse):

1. Using your first two or three fingers (not your thumb—it has a pulse of its own and could mislead you), press lightly on the neck just to the side of the Adam's apple. (Feel for a slight groove between the Adam's apple and the neck muscle.) Feel for the pulse on the side of the neck closer to you. Do not reach across the child's throat. Be sure to give yourself up to ten seconds to find your child's pulse. While you are finding your child's pulse, remember to keep his head tilted back slightly so that his airway remains open.

2. If you find your child's pulse, go back and check his breathing again. Since he has a pulse, this means his heart is beating and his blood is cir-

culating. But he still may not be breathing on his own. If this is the case, you must continue to breathe for him!

Note: If your child has *no pulse,* you must begin CPR immediately! (See Part II, "CPR! Breathing for Your Child and Doing Chest Compressions," page 58).

Learning to find your child's pulse is the only thing you as a parent can practice on your child before a life-threatening emergency happens. **Never practice any lifesaving technique in this book on any living thing.** *At BABY-LIFE the importance of parents' knowing how to take their child's pulse is continually stressed. If you have trouble locating your child's pulse when you practice, ask your pediatrician to help you.*

FINDING THE PULSE

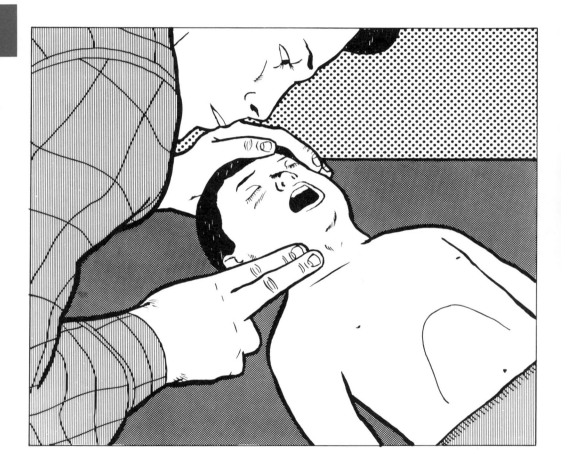

USE YOUR FIRST TWO OR THREE FINGERS

Find your child's pulse with your first two or three fingers. Don't use your thumb—it has a pulse of its own.

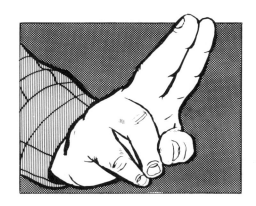

FIND YOUR CHILD'S CAROTID PULSE

Your child's carotid pulse is located in the neck, on either side of the Adam's apple.

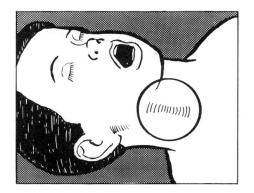

PRESS LIGHTLY ON THE NECK, JUST TO THE SIDE OF THE ADAM'S APPLE

Feel for the pulse on the side of the neck closer to you. Do not reach across your child's throat. Give yourself up to ten seconds to locate the pulse. (If child has a pulse, see p. 28. If child has no pulse, see p. 32.)

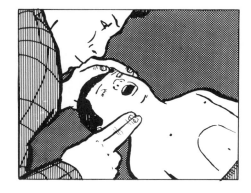

BREATHING FOR YOUR CHILD

"THE BREATH OF LIFE"

If your child has a pulse but does not start breathing on his own after you give him the first two breaths, *you must begin breathing for your child regularly to keep him supplied with oxygen.*

BREATHE FOR YOUR CHILD (at approximately the same rate he would breathe if he were able to do it on his own):

1. While keeping the airway open by lifting the chin and tilting the head back slightly, pinch your child's nose with your thumb and index finger and cover your child's mouth with your mouth, making an airtight seal. Blow a *slow* breath into your child. Blow only long enough and with just enough force to make his chest rise. *Remember to look out of the corner of your eye each time you blow a breath into him to see his chest rise.* Then take your mouth off your child and release the nose to let the air out of him.

2. Once again make an airtight seal by pinching your child's nose and covering your child's mouth with your mouth. Blow another slow breath into your child, only long enough and with just enough force to make his chest rise. Remember to take your mouth off your child and release his nose after each breath in order to let the air out of him and to take a breath yourself.

3. Breathe into your child as regularly as you can—one breath every four seconds (at least fifteen breaths per minute). Count out loud: "One thousand one, one thousand two, one thousand three"—*breathe!* Counting out loud keeps you focused and can help control panic. It forces you to concentrate and to breathe normally, and can prevent you from hyperventilating. Keep in mind that you are actually breathing for your child! If you stop, he will have no air.

4. After one minute (about fifteen breaths), stop and check your child's pulse and breathing. Use your first two or three fingers (not your thumb) and press *lightly* on the side of the neck closer to you.

If his pulse is still there, check for breathing. If he has not yet started to breathe on his own, keep breathing for him until he breathes on his own, or until emergency medical help arrives.

Note: *If, after one minute* of breathing for your child, no one has answered your cries for help, come to your aid, or summoned emergency medical help, you must continue your lifesaving efforts, but now *YOU MUST GET HELP* yourself by calling **911** or your local Emergency Medical Services (EMS) number. While you are waiting for help to arrive, *continue breathing for your child*. Every minute or so, check for your child's pulse and to see if he has started to breathe on his own. If your child does start breathing on his own, but remains unconscious, you must *still keep his airway open* and continue to watch him closely to make sure he keeps breathing and has a pulse. (See Part IV, "How to Get Emergency Medical Help!" page 106.)

BREATHING FOR YOUR CHILD

BLOW A SLOW BREATH INTO YOUR CHILD

Pinch your child's nose and cover his mouth with your mouth, and make an airtight seal. Blow a *slow* breath into him, just enough to make his chest rise. Look out of the corner of your eye as you blow a breath in to be sure your child's chest rises.

TAKE YOUR MOUTH OFF YOUR CHILD

Take your mouth off the child and release his nose to let the air out of him and to take another breath yourself.

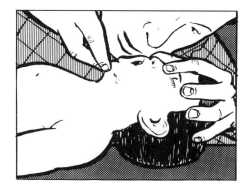

BLOW ANOTHER SLOW BREATH INTO YOUR CHILD

Continue to breathe into your child—one breath every four seconds—taking your mouth off your child and releasing his nose between breaths to let the air out of him and to take another breath yourself.

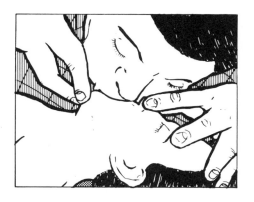

CPR! BREATHING FOR YOUR CHILD AND DOING CHEST COMPRESSIONS

NO PULSE! If your child has no pulse, that means his heart has stopped beating and there is no circulation. *YOU MUST BEGIN CPR IMMEDIATELY!*

You must do the work of the heart and the lungs by performing CPR—cardiopulmonary resuscitation. Now you will not only breathe for your child, you will do the pumping for his heart as well.

*YOU DO CPR FOR ONE REASON ONLY—NO PULSE—*and you are the one who will have to determine if your child has no pulse and whether you must do CPR. To avoid doing CPR unnecessarily, learn how to find your child's pulse and practice finding it *before* an emergency happens!

CPR HAS RISKS! Even doing it correctly, you could do damage to your child. If you do it wrong, you could do irreversible damage! However, if your child has stopped breathing, and you cannot find his pulse, then *CPR COULD*

SAVE HIS LIFE! But you must do it right.

When you do CPR, you will be pressing on your child's sternum. (The sternum is the breastbone, which runs down the center of the chest.) You must press *exactly* in the right place. If you push too low on the sternum you can cause serious, even fatal, injury. At the bottom tip of the sternum is a fragile piece of cartilage called the *xiphoid process.* If pressed, this triangular-shaped cartilage could scrape or lacerate the liver and cause severe internal bleeding. On either side of the sternum are the ribs. If you press directly on the child's ribs, you could easily break or splinter a rib, which could puncture a lung or other vital organ. Pressing too high on the sternum or using jabbing or poking motions to compress the sternum could also be dangerous, and you might not be effective in circulating the blood carrying precious oxygen to the brain.

Don't forget, if the brain isn't supplied with oxygen, irreversible damage will occur after four to six minutes. So if CPR is *delayed,* or if you do CPR *improperly,* even if your child is revived he could still be seriously impaired.

This is why you *must* be properly

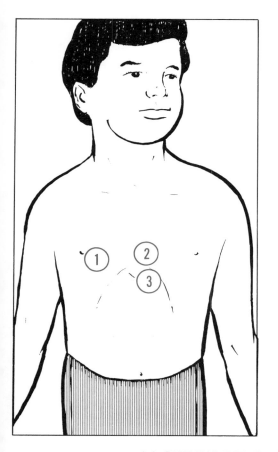 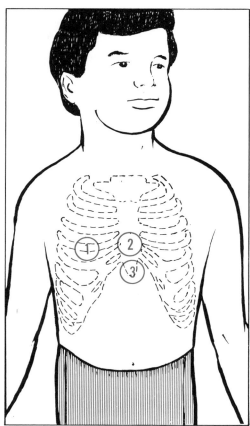

(1) CHILD'S RIB CAGE (DO NOT PRESS)
(2) STERNUM
(3) XIPHOID PROCESS (DO NOT PRESS)

trained to do CPR in a course given by certified instructors, where you will learn the techniques by practicing on mannequins. Practice CPR only on dolls or mannequins, *never* on any living thing!

Remember the steps before starting CPR: Carefully supporting the child's head, neck, and body, place him on his back. Open the airway by lifting the chin and tilting the head back slightly (this moves the tongue off the windpipe). Check to see whether your child is breathing. If he is not, blow two slow breaths into him, making the chest rise each time, and removing your mouth between breaths. Then feel for his pulse for up to ten seconds. Use your first two or three fingers—not your thumb—and press *lightly* on the neck just to the side of the Adam's apple.

IF YOU FIND NO PULSE AFTER TEN SECONDS, BEGIN CPR:

1. Make sure the child is on a firm, flat surface such as the floor. You cannot do CPR effectively on a soft surface such as a bed or sofa!

2. Place one hand on your child's forehead, keeping his head tilted back *slightly* to keep his airway open.

Use your other hand, the one closer to the child's feet, to locate the correct place on the sternum to do CPR compressions. With your middle finger, lightly trace along the inside edge of the rib cage nearer to you, just up to the notch where the ribs come together at the sternum. *DO NOT PRESS!*

3. Rest your middle finger lightly on the notch, and put your index finger next to it.

4. Carefully *note the exact location of the index finger*. Now lift both fingers and immediately place the heel of your hand *just above* where your index finger was. The heel of your hand should now be on the sternum, about two fingers' width above the xiphoid process, in the correct position to begin chest compressions. Bend your fingers back, so only the heel of your hand is touching the sternum and *you are not pressing on the ribs*. See illustration for the correct placement of the heel of your hand.

5. Position yourself over the center of your child's chest. Keeping your arm straight and your elbow

locked, use the *heel of your hand* and press the sternum straight down, one inch to one and a half inches, and release all the way, leaving the heel of your hand resting lightly in place on the sternum. Continue to press and release, being careful not to lift the heel of your hand off the chest or press on the ribs. Count out loud: "One, *and* two, *and* three, *and* four, *and* five." (Press down on the count and release on the "and.") You will be doing slightly more than one compression per second.

6. After five compressions stop pumping, and making sure your child's airway is open, pinch his nose, make an airtight seal over your child's mouth with your mouth, and blow a slow breath into him. *Blow into your child only long enough and with just enough force to make his chest rise.* Release his nose and take your mouth off your child's mouth to let the air out of him.

7. Give your child five more chest compressions. Each compression should be done smoothly. Spend equal time compressing and releas-

ing. *Do not poke or jab your child.* Keep your arm straight, your elbow locked, and your hand bent back at the wrist while you are doing the compressions. Use only the heel of your hand, making sure your fingers do not touch the ribs. Remember to press straight down, not at an angle. *NEVER PRESS ON THE XIPHOID PROCESS!*

8. After every five compressions, blow a slow breath into your child, just enough to make his chest rise.

While you are doing CPR for a child, you may have to move the heel of your hand off the sternum to reopen his airway each time you breathe for him. Before you begin the compressions again, remember to reposition the heel of your hand correctly.

Continue the compressions and breathing for your child for one minute. Then stop. Try to find his pulse and check for his breathing. If you find no pulse or breathing, continue CPR. *CHECK FOR THE PULSE AND THE BREATHING EVERY MINUTE OR SO!* If you find the pulse stop the chest compressions. But if your child has not yet started to breathe on his own, *you must keep breathing for him* (one breath every four seconds). If your child starts breathing on his own but remains unconscious, *be sure to keep his airway open* and continue to check his pulse and breathing until help arrives.

Remember: Whether you are only breathing for your child or doing both breathing and chest compressions, *if no one has come to your aid after one minute, continue your lifesaving efforts and GET HELP!* Call **911** or your local Emergency Medical Services number. (See Part IV, "How to Get Emergency Medical Help!" page 106.)

GETTING READY TO DO CHEST COMPRESSIONS

LIGHTLY TRACE ALONG THE INSIDE EDGE OF THE RIB CAGE

With your middle finger, lightly trace along the inside edge of the rib cage on the side nearer to you, just up to the notch where the ribs come together at the sternum.

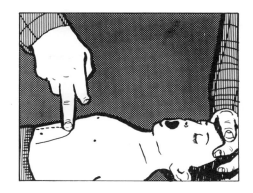

PUT YOUR INDEX FINGER NEXT TO YOUR MIDDLE FINGER

Rest your middle finger lightly on the notch, and put your index finger next to it on the sternum.

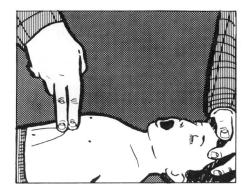

PLACE THE HEEL OF YOUR HAND JUST ABOVE WHERE YOUR INDEX FINGER WAS

Carefully note the exact location of the index finger. Now lift both fingers and place the heel of your hand just *above* where your index finger was. Bend your fingers back so only the heel of your hand is touching the sternum.

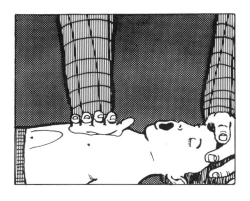

DOING CHEST COMPRESSIONS AND BREATHING FOR YOUR CHILD

PRESS THE STERNUM STRAIGHT DOWN

Keeping your arm straight and your elbow locked, use the heel of your hand and press the sternum straight down, one inch to one and a half inches. (Do not press on the xiphoid process.)

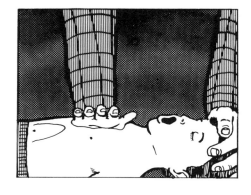

RELEASE ALL THE WAY

Release the sternum completely, leaving the heel of your hand resting lightly in place. Press and release the sternum again. Do a total of five compressions.

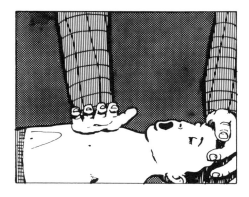

BLOW A SLOW BREATH INTO YOUR CHILD

After five compressions, making sure your child's airway is open, pinch his nose and make an airtight seal with your mouth over the child's mouth. Blow a slow breath into your child, just enough to make his chest rise. Keep repeating five chest compressions, *and* to give a slow breath after every fifth compression.

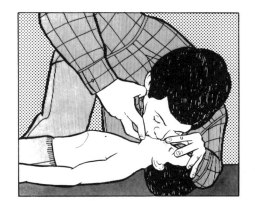

Part III

Lifesaving Information: Clearing an Obstructed Airway

IS YOUR CHILD REALLY CHOKING?

You are feeding your baby and the phone rings. You are about to make two serious mistakes . . .

You leave the baby alone while he is eating to answer the phone. You leave food within his reach that is not properly mashed or shredded—food he could choke on!

While your back is turned, your baby stuffs all the food on his plate into his mouth, and chokes! Because his airway is obstructed, your baby can't cry or make a noise. Even though you are close by, you don't hear anything. Within minutes your baby becomes unconscious. . . .

If you ever leave your baby alone while he is eating, this could happen— he could choke and become unconscious within minutes!

Choking is every parent's number-one fear. It is the single most anxiety-provoking topic in the BABY-LIFE classes. And since statistics indicate that it is a leading cause of death in infants and young children (one child chokes to death every five days), you must know exactly what to do if your child is choking. You must also be able to recognize when your child *is* choking and needs your immediate help, and when he is *not!*

If your child starts to cough while you're feeding him, your first instinct may be to hit him on his back. Or you might immediately stick your fingers into his mouth without even seeing what is in there. Or you might panic and turn him upside down.

Parents do all these things, and yet all of them have serious risks and are probably unnecessary. If your child has a good strong cough and is turning red, he is doing the best possible thing: He is attempting to clear his throat himself. *Coughing is your child's natural reflex to clear something that is irritating his throat.* It is also the most effective thing he can do for himself. If your child is able to cough forcefully, it means he is able to breathe—*he has good air exchange.* Also, if he is turning red, it means there is plenty of oxygen in his blood.

When your child is coughing and trying to clear his throat, don't interfere. *Encourage him to continue coughing.* To encourage a baby, cough yourself. Babies love to imitate, and if you start to cough he will do what you are doing. For an older child, have him raise his arms. When he raises his arms it makes it easier for him to cough more effectively, and it also seems to reassure the child. (Keeping your child calm is important—fear can actually cause his throat to constrict.)

When an infant is coughing (on formula, for instance), very *gently* pat him on the back and reassure him. If he is coughing effectively, don't interfere with his efforts.

If you do something too aggressive, such as forcefully slapping your child's back (especially if he is upright), you may actually drive whatever is in his mouth farther back into his throat!

If you blindly reach into your child's mouth with your fingers *without seeing what you are reaching for*, you could push whatever is causing him to cough farther back into his throat and windpipe.

Turning a baby upside down can frighten him and cause him to stop coughing. Even worse, if there is something in his throat, it could become more firmly lodged. You also risk dropping him!

Doing any one of these things while your child is able to cough effectively might cause a choking problem where there was none to begin with!

Caution: Even though coughing is a sign that there is good air exchange and your child is doing the best possible thing, *persistent, unrelieved* coughing or noisy breathing could indicate illness or a more serious problem (a small object could have been inhaled into the lung). For persistent coughing, get medical advice immediately!

There are *times, however, when your child could be choking.* His airway might be obstructed by a foreign object, and he will need your immediate help. You may actually see your child put something in his mouth and start to choke, or you may suspect his airway is obstructed because of the circumstances: He was playing with a small toy or eating, and now he is having difficulty breathing, or you find him unconscious. The physical signs that tell you your child is *really choking* are:

- He will be unable to cough, or he will have a *weak, ineffective* cough.

- He won't be able to talk or cry.

- He will have difficulty breathing.

- You might hear a high-pitched crowing noise when he attempts to breathe.

- Color will drain from his face.

- His lips may become pale, grayish, or even blue. (With a dark-skinned child, you will more easily see a color change in the fingernail beds.)

- An older child might clutch his throat, the universal distress signal for choking.

- You may find your child unconscious and not breathing, and his chest doesn't rise when you attempt to breathe for him.

If you see any of these signs, *your child's airway is obstructed!* He is not getting enough air (poor air exchange). This is a life-threatening emergency! You must take immediate steps to save your child's life!

Caution: Very often illnesses such as croup or epiglottitis can cause breathing difficulties. You might see some of the same signs in your child as you would if he were choking on food or a toy. However, you can tell the difference because when something like food or a toy obstructs the airway, it happens suddenly, unlike an illness, which gives you some advance warning (a fever, a sore throat, congestion).

If a baby or young child has *any* upper respiratory illness, even a bad cold, *call your pediatrician*, follow his or her instructions carefully and, just as important, *watch your child closely.* Parents at BABY-LIFE frequently ask whether this means they have to watch their child all night long. The answer is *yes!* Upper respiratory infections frequently get worse in the middle of the night. This means you must monitor him throughout the night, checking on him frequently. If symptoms get worse, get immediate medical help before the illness becomes life-threatening.

A *severe allergic reaction* might also block your child's airway. This could happen much more quickly than an illness. However, you would see signs and symptoms—such as hives, swelling, itching, a rash, or wheezing. You should get medical advice for *any* allergic reaction. If your child is having breathing difficulties due to an allergic reaction, don't waste any time. *Get emergency medical help immediately!*

INFANT/BABY (NEWBORN TO ONE YEAR)

YOUR BABY IS CHOKING!

If your baby is coughing forcefully and he can breathe normally, he has *good air exchange*. The best thing you can do for him is to keep him calm, watch him closely, and encourage his efforts.

If, however, he is trying to cough but can't, or if he has a weak, ineffective cough, if he can't talk or cry, and is having difficulty breathing, then your baby is choking! You must act immediately to save him!

DO BACK BLOWS AND CHEST THRUSTS TO RELIEVE THE OB-STRUCTION:

1. Turn your baby face down and slide your arm under his body. Support his head by cupping your hand around his jaw, not the soft tissue of the neck. Your baby will now be straddling your arm. Rest your arm on your thigh to help support the weight of the baby. Keep the baby's head lower than his body. Gravity may help dislodge the object.
   Note: If your baby is too heavy for you to support him comfortably with your arm resting on your thigh, *drape the baby directly across your lap.* Remember to keep his head lower than his body and support his head and neck.

2. Deliver four back blows between your baby's shoulder blades with the heel of your hand. Careful! Be sure the back blows are delivered directly between the shoulder blades and *adjust the force you use to the size of the baby.*

3. If, after you deliver the back blows, the obstruction has not been cleared, do four chest thrusts. Gently place your hand on the back of the baby's head, sandwiching him between both arms. Continue to support his head and neck. Carefully turn him over onto his back and rest him on your other thigh, keeping his head lower than his body, if possible.

4. Place your two fingers on the sternum (breastbone) in exactly the

same position as when doing the chest compressions for CPR, one finger's width below the center of an imaginary line drawn between the nipples.

5.   Give your baby four chest thrusts, pressing straight down on the sternum with two or three fingers and releasing each time. Keep your fingers resting lightly on the sternum between chest thrusts. (These chest thrusts are being done to expel the obstruction. They are performed in the same manner as for CPR, but slightly slower.)
Caution: Do not press on the bottom tip of the sternum (the xiphoid process) or the ribs.

6.   After doing the four chest thrusts, again sandwich your baby between both arms while continuing to support his head and neck. Carefully turn him over onto his chest and support him on your other thigh, with his head lower than his body. Repeat the four back blows between the shoulder blades with the heel of your hand. Alternate the four back blows with the four chest thrusts. Try to remove the object with your fingers *only if you can*

see it and can get it out without pushing it farther back in.

You will know the obstruction is cleared if you see it come out, if your baby starts crying or coughing, or if he starts breathing normally and his color improves.
Even if you are successful in clearing the obstruction, your baby should be taken to an emergency medical facility to check for further complications!

If Your Baby Becomes Unconscious . . .

If you are not successful in clearing the obstruction, *your baby may become unconscious.* If he becomes unconscious, *YELL FOR HELP!* Get someone to call **911** or your local Emergency Medical Services number. Since your baby is unconscious, the muscles of his throat have relaxed and you may now be successful in clearing the obstruction:

1.   Carefully place your baby on his back. Before continuing the back blows and chest thrusts, look into your baby's mouth to see if the ob-

ject is now visible and can be removed. Open his mouth, depress his tongue with your thumb, and pull his tongue and jaw forward with your fingers hooked under his chin. This pulls the tongue away from the back of the throat and may help dislodge an object that is stuck there.

2. Try to remove the object only if you can see it and can get it out without pushing it farther back into your baby's throat.

3. Since your baby is unconscious and *not breathing*, now you must also try to breathe for him! When attempting to breathe for your baby, remember to open the airway by lifting his chin and tilting his head back slightly.

If you are unable to get air into your baby and make his chest rise, this means his airway is still obstructed! *Repeat the back blows and chest thrusts!* Continue to check to see whether the object is visible and can be removed. Keep trying to blow air into your baby and make his chest rise! *BE PERSISTENT!*

If at any time the object is expelled, you are able to remove it, or you are able to breathe into your baby and make his chest rise, *his airway is cleared!* However, if he remains unconscious and does not start breathing on his own, you will have to keep breathing for him! You must also check his pulse. *If he has no pulse, you will now have to do CPR!*

Caution: Your baby could vomit at any time, before or during any lifesaving procedure for choking. If he is unconscious, you must turn him on his side immediately and clean out his mouth to keep his airway and lungs clear.

Important Note: There is some disagreement among medical authorities as to the *best* way to clear an infant's obstructed airway. Although the current medical guidelines recommend a combination of back blows and chest thrusts, some doctors disagree.

Parents should check with their own pediatrician to get his or her recommendations, and should regularly take CPR courses to stay up to date on the methods for clearing an obstructed airway.

DELIVERING BACK BLOWS TO RELIEVE AN OBSTRUCTION

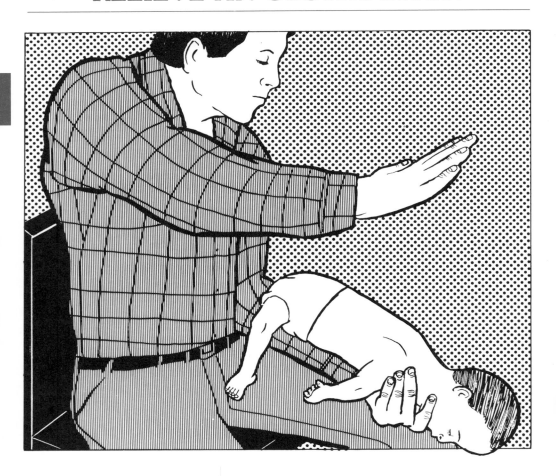

SLIDE YOUR ARM UNDER YOUR BABY'S BODY

With your baby face down, slide your arm under his body, and support his head by cupping his jaw with your hand. Your baby will now be straddling your arm. (Drape your baby across your lap if he is too heavy to straddle your arm.)

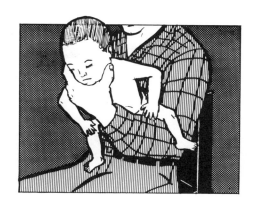

SUPPORT YOUR BABY ON YOUR THIGH, KEEPING HIS HEAD LOWER THAN HIS BODY

You will be using the heel of your hand to deliver back blows directly between your baby's shoulder blades.

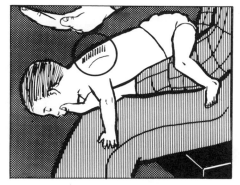

DELIVER FOUR BACK BLOWS BETWEEN YOUR BABY'S SHOULDER BLADES

Adjust the force of the blows to the size of your baby. (If back blows do not relieve the obstruction, try chest thrusts. See next page.)

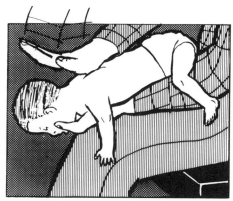

DOING CHEST THRUSTS
TO RELIEVE AN OBSTRUCTION

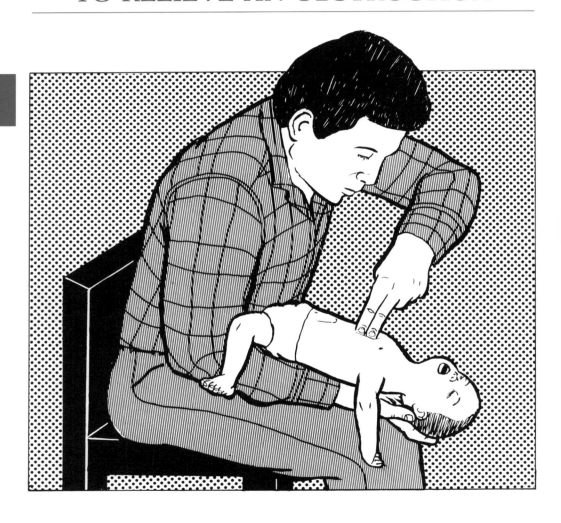

SANDWICH YOUR BABY BETWEEN BOTH ARMS

Gently place your hand on the back of your baby's head and support his head and neck.

TURN YOUR BABY OVER ON HIS BACK

Carefully turn him over onto his back, and support him on your other thigh, keeping his head lower than his body, if possible.

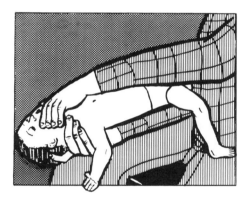

GIVE YOUR BABY FOUR CHEST THRUSTS

Place two fingers on the sternum, just below the nipple line, in exactly the same position as when doing chest compressions for CPR. Give your baby four chest thrusts, pressing straight down on the sternum and releasing each time. (Do not press on the xiphoid process.) Repeat back blows and chest thrusts until the obstruction is cleared.

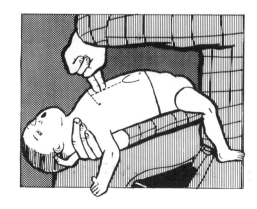

RELIEVING THE OBSTRUCTION
IF BABY BECOMES UNCONSCIOUS

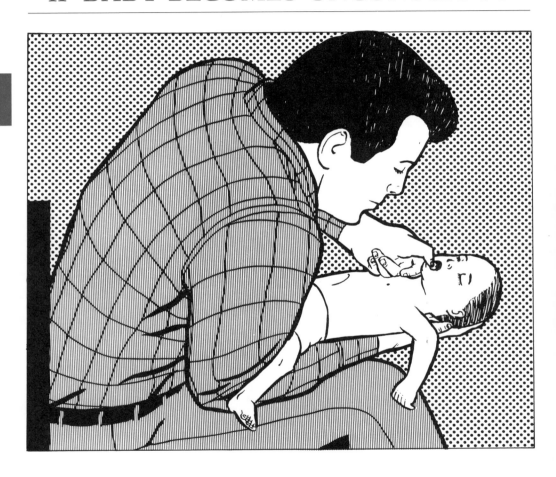

OPEN YOUR BABY'S MOUTH AND LOOK IN

If your baby becomes unconscious, open his mouth, depress his tongue with your thumb, and pull his tongue forward with your fingers hooked under his chin. Look to see if the object is visible.

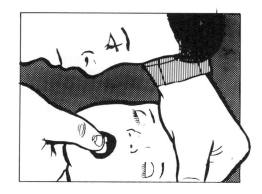

IF YOU SEE AN OBSTRUCTION, REMOVE IT

Try to remove the object only *if you can see it* and can get it out without pushing it farther back into your baby's throat.

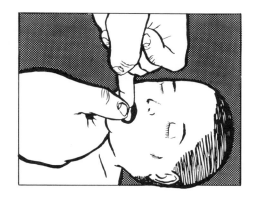

BREATHE FOR YOUR BABY

Since your baby is unconscious and not breathing, now you must also try to breathe for him. If you blow air into the baby and his chest does not rise, repeat the back blows and chest thrusts. Continue to check to see if the object is visible and can be removed. Keep trying to blow air into your baby and make his chest rise.

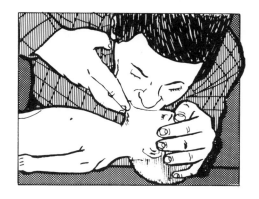

YOUR BABY IS UNCONSCIOUS! HIS AIRWAY IS OBSTRUCTED

If you found your baby unconscious and not breathing, you wouldn't necessarily know the reason why! He might have choked and become unconscious, but if you didn't see it happen you wouldn't know for sure until you opened his airway and tried to breathe for him.

Remember that the first thing you must do when you find your baby is try to wake him up—pat and nudge or pinch your baby gently. If he doesn't respond, *YELL FOR HELP!* Get someone to call **911** or your local Emergency Medical Services number.

Then take care of the *AIRWAY, BREATHING, CIRCULATION:*

1. Carefully supporting his head, neck, and body, place your baby on his back. Open his airway by lifting his chin and tilting his head back *slightly* (to get his tongue out of the way). Check to see if your baby is breathing. If he is not breathing, *you must try to breathe for him!*

2. Put your mouth over your baby's mouth and nose, make an airtight seal, and blow a *slow* breath into him. As you blow, watch out of the corner of your eye to see whether your baby's chest rises. If your baby's airway is obstructed, you will be unable to make his chest rise.

3. If you are not successful in making his chest rise the first time, tilt his head again, lift his chin, and try a second time to breathe into him. Do this to make sure his tongue is not still obstructing his airway.

If you are still unable to blow air into your baby and make his chest rise, *his airway may be blocked by a foreign object.* You must try to clear the obstruction.

USE A COMBINATION OF BACK BLOWS AND CHEST THRUSTS:

1. Turn your baby face down and slide your arm under his body. Support his head by cupping your hand around his jaw, not the soft tissue of the neck. Your baby will now be

straddling your arm. Rest your arm on your thigh to help support the weight of the baby. Keep the baby's head lower than his body. Gravity may help dislodge the object.

Note: If your baby is too heavy for you to support him comfortably with your arm resting on your thigh, *drape the baby directly across your lap.* Remember to keep his head lower than his body and to support his head and neck.

2. Deliver four back blows between your baby's shoulder blades with the heel of your hand. Careful! Be sure the back blows are delivered directly between the shoulder blades, and adjust the force you use to the size of the baby.

3. If, after you deliver the back blows, the obstruction has not been cleared, do four chest thrusts. Gently place your hand on the back of your baby's head, sandwiching him between both arms. Continue to support his head and neck. Carefully turn him over onto his back and rest him on your other thigh, keeping his head lower than his body, if possible.

4. Place your two fingers on the sternum (breastbone) in exactly the same position as when doing the chest compressions for CPR, one finger's width below the center of an imaginary line drawn between the nipples.

5. Give your baby four chest thrusts, pressing straight down on the sternum with two or three fingers and releasing each time. Keep your fingers resting lightly on the sternum between chest thrusts. (These chest thrusts are being done to expel the obstruction. They are performed in the same manner as for CPR, but slightly slower.)

   Caution: Do not press on the bottom tip of the sternum (the xiphoid process) or on the ribs.

6. After doing the four chest thrusts, *look into your baby's mouth to see if the object is visible.* Open your baby's mouth. Depress his tongue with your thumb and pull his lower jaw forward with your fingers. Try to remove the object only if you can see it and get it out without pushing it farther back into your baby's throat.

7. If your baby is still unconscious and has not yet started breathing, *you must now try again to get air into him!*

If you are still unable to get air into your baby and make his chest rise, *repeat the back blows and chest thrusts!* Continue to check to see whether the object is visible and can be removed. Keep trying to blow air into the baby and make his chest rise. *BE PERSISTENT!*

If at any time the object is expelled, you are able to remove it, or you are able to breathe into your baby and make his chest rise, *his airway is cleared!* However, if he remains unconscious and does not start breathing on his own, you will have to keep breathing for him! You must also check his pulse. If he has no pulse, *you will now have to do CPR!*

YOUR BABY IS UNCONSCIOUS!

OPEN YOUR BABY'S AIRWAY

With your baby lying flat, open his airway by lifting his chin and tilting his head back *slightly*.

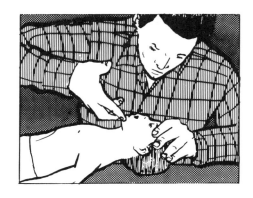

CHECK HIS BREATHING

Check to see if your baby is breathing. If he is not breathing, you must *try* to breathe for him.

BREATHE FOR YOUR BABY

Put your mouth over your baby's mouth and nose, and blow a slow breath into him. If his chest does not rise, reposition his head and try again. If it still does not rise, *the airway may be obstructed by a foreign object.*

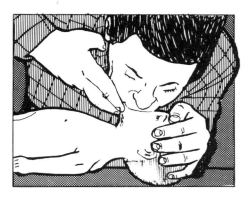

HIS AIRWAY IS OBSTRUCTED

DELIVER FOUR BACK BLOWS TO DISLODGE THE OBJECT

With your baby supported on your thigh, and his head lower than his body, deliver four back blows between his shoulder blades with the heel of your hand. Adjust the force of the blows to the size of the baby.

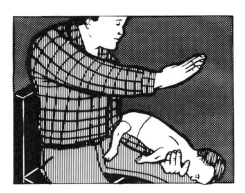

GIVE YOUR BABY FOUR CHEST THRUSTS TO EXPEL OBJECT

Turn your baby onto his back, and place your two fingers on the sternum in exactly the same position as when doing chest compressions for CPR. Give your baby four chest thrusts, pressing straight down and releasing each time. (Do not press on the xiphoid process.)

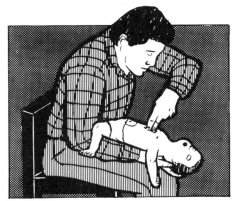

LOOK FOR THE OBJECT. TRY TO BLOW A BREATH INTO YOUR BABY

If you can see the object and can get it out without pushing it farther back, try to remove it. *Try again to get air into your baby.* If you are still unable to make his chest rise, repeat the back blows and chest thrusts. Continue to check if the object is visible. Try to blow air into the baby.

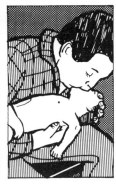

CHILD (ONE YEAR TO EIGHT YEARS)

YOUR CHILD IS CHOKING!

The signs you will see if your child is choking on a foreign object are the same as for a baby. However, the techniques you will use to save him are different!

If your child is coughing forcefully and he can breathe normally, he has *good air exchange.* The best thing you can do for him is to keep him calm, watch him closely, and encourage his efforts.

If, however, he is trying to cough but can't, or if he has a weak, ineffective cough, if he can't talk or cry and is having difficulty breathing, then your child is choking! You must act immediately to save him!

USE THE HEIMLICH MANEUVER:

1. Position yourself behind your child so that his back is against you for support. Wrap your arms around his midsection, being careful to keep your arms off the child's ribs.

2. Make a fist. Place the thumb side of your fist against the child's abdomen, slightly *above* the navel.
Caution: *Not too high!* Stay below the xiphoid process and rib cage!

3. Clasp your fist with your other hand. Pull your fist into your child's abdomen with a quick *upward* thrust. *Adjust the force of the thrust to the size of the child.* Make sure the thrust is delivered to the center of your child's abdomen and not to either side. Do not press on your child's ribs with your arms. You may have to do several thrusts. Any one of the thrusts could dislodge the object. Try to remove the object with your fingers *only if you can see it* and can get it out without pushing it farther back in.

You will know the obstruction is cleared if you see it come out, if your child starts crying or coughing, or if he starts breathing normally and his color improves.

Even if you are successful in clearing the obstruction, your child should be taken to an emergency medical facility to check for any further complications!

If Your Child Becomes Unconscious . . .

If you are not successful in clearing the obstruction, *your child may become unconscious.* If he becomes unconscious, *YELL FOR HELP!* Get someone to call **911** or your local Emergency Medical Services number. Since your child is unconscious, the muscles of his throat have relaxed and you may now be successful in clearing the obstruction.

1. Carefully place your child on his back. Before continuing the Heimlich maneuver, look into your child's mouth to see if the object is now visible and can be removed. Open his mouth, depress his tongue with your thumb, and pull his jaw forward with your fingers hooked under his chin. This pulls the tongue away from the back of the throat and may help dislodge any object that is stuck there.

2. Try to remove the object only if you can see it and can get it out without pushing it farther back into your child's throat.

3. Since your child is unconscious and *not breathing*, now you must

also try to breathe for him! When attempting to breathe for your child, remember to open the airway by lifting his chin and tilting his head back slightly.

If you are unable to get air into your child and make his chest rise, this means his airway is still obstructed! You will have to repeat the Heimlich maneuver, but since your child is now unconscious and lying on his back, *you will have to do the Heimlich maneuver a different way:*

1. Kneel at your child's feet and place the heel of one hand on your child's abdomen, slightly *above* the navel. *Remember to stay below the xiphoid process and the rib cage!*

2. Place your other hand directly on top of the first hand and interlace your fingers. Bend your fingers back so only the heel of your hand is in place on the abdomen. (See illustration for the correct position of your hand and fingers.)

3. Press into the abdomen with a quick *upward* thrust. Make sure the thrust is *not* delivered off to either side. You may have to do several

thrusts. Any one of the thrusts could dislodge the object.

Careful! With a small child the thrusts should be done gently. Always adjust the force of the thrust to the size of the child.

4. After doing several thrusts, look into your child's mouth to see if the object is now visible and can be removed.

5. If the child has not yet started breathing, *you must try again to get air into him!*

If you are still unable to get air into your child and make his chest rise, re-peat *the Heimlich maneuver!* Continue to check to see whether the object is visible and can be removed. Keep trying to blow air into your child and make his chest rise! *BE PERSISTENT!*

If at any time the object is expelled, you are able to remove it, or you are able to breathe into your child and make his chest rise, *his airway is cleared!* However, if he remains unconscious and does not start breathing on his own, you will have to keep breathing for him! You must also check his pulse. *If he has no pulse, you will now have to do CPR!*

Caution: Your child could vomit at any time before or during any lifesaving procedure for choking. If he is uncon-scious, you must turn him on his side immediately and clean out his mouth to keep his airway and lungs clear.

USING THE HEIMLICH MANEUVER TO RELIEVE AN OBSTRUCTION

POSITION YOURSELF BEHIND YOUR CHILD, SO HIS BACK IS AGAINST YOU FOR SUPPORT

Wrap your arms around his midsection, being careful to keep your arms off your child's ribs.

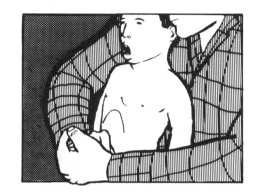

MAKE A FIST

You will be placing the thumb side of your fist against your child's abdomen, slightly *above* the navel. Don't touch the ribs or xiphoid process.

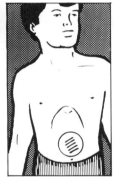

CLASP YOUR FIST WITH YOUR OTHER HAND, AND PULL INTO YOUR CHILD'S ABDOMEN

Use a quick, *upward* thrust, and make sure the thrust is delivered to the center of the abdomen, not to either side. Do not press on your child's ribs with your arms. Adjust the force of the thrust to the size of the child. You may have to do several thrusts. Any one of the thrusts could dislodge the object.

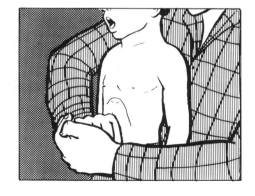

RELIEVING THE OBSTRUCTION IF THE CHILD BECOMES UNCONSCIOUS

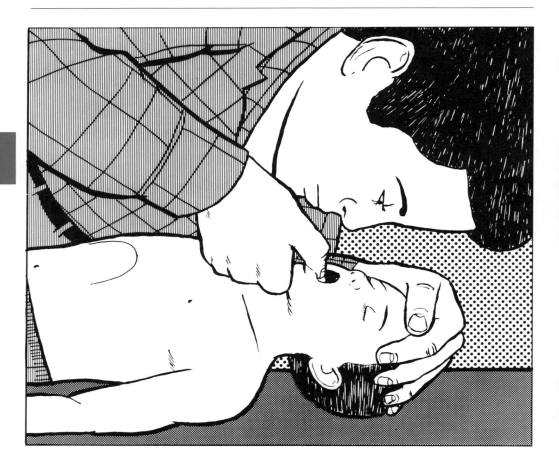

OPEN YOUR CHILD'S MOUTH AND LOOK IN

If your child becomes unconscious, open his mouth, depress his tongue with your thumb, and pull his jaw forward with your fingers hooked under his chin. Look to see if the object is visible.

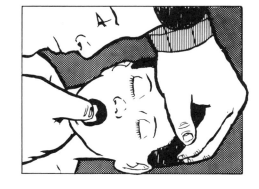

IF YOU SEE AN OBSTRUCTION, REMOVE IT

Try to remove the object *only if you can see it* and can get it out without pushing it farther back into your child's throat.

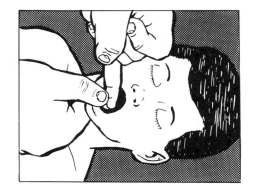

BREATHE FOR YOUR CHILD

Since your child is unconscious and not breathing, now you must also try to breathe for him. If you are unable to make his chest rise, *do the Heimlich maneuver for an unconscious child* (see next page).

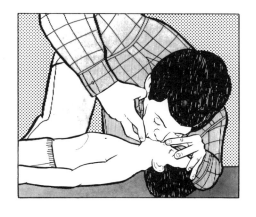

DOING THE HEIMLICH MANEUVER FOR AN UNCONSCIOUS CHILD

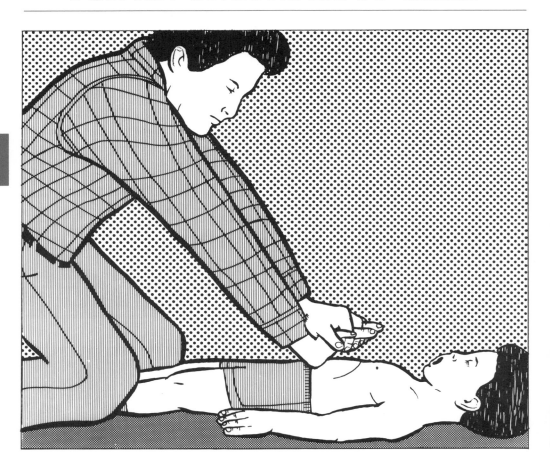

USE THE HEEL OF ONE HAND

You will be using the heel of one hand, with the fingers bent back, to do the Heimlich maneuver for an unconscious child.

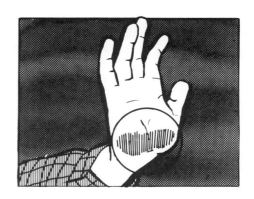

PLACE THE HEEL OF ONE HAND ON YOUR CHILD'S ABDOMEN

Kneel at your child's feet and place the heel of one hand on his abdomen, slightly above the navel, but below the xiphoid process and not touching the ribs.

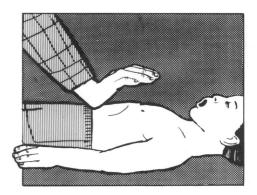

PRESS INTO THE ABDOMEN WITH AN UPWARD THRUST

Place your other hand on top and interlace your fingers. Press into the abdomen with a quick *upward* thrust. Adjust the force you use to the size of the child. Make sure the thrust is not delivered to either side. Repeat the Heimlich maneuver. Continue to check if the object is visible and can be removed. Keep trying to blow air into your child and make his chest rise.

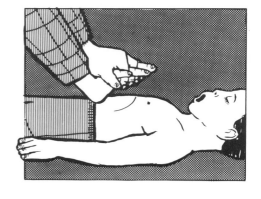

YOUR CHILD IS UNCONSCIOUS! HIS AIRWAY IS OBSTRUCTED

If you found your child unconscious and not breathing, you wouldn't necessarily know the reason why. He might have choked and become unconscious, but if you didn't see it happen you wouldn't know for sure until you opened his airway and tried to breathe for him.

Remember that the first thing you must do when you find your child is try to wake him up—pat and nudge or pinch your child gently. If he doesn't respond, *YELL FOR HELP!* Get someone to call **911** or your local Emergency Medical Services number.

Then, take care of *AIRWAY, BREATHING, CIRCULATION:*

1. Carefully supporting his head, neck, and body, place your child on his back. Open his airway by lifting his chin and tilting his head back *slightly* (to get his tongue out of the way). Check to see if your child is breathing. If he is not breathing, *you must try to breathe for him!*

2. Pinch your child's nose and put your mouth over his mouth, making an airtight seal, and blow a *slow* breath into him. As you blow, watch out of the corner of your eye to see whether your child's chest rises. If your child's airway is obstructed, you will be unable to make his chest rise.

3. If you are not successful in making his chest rise the first time, tilt his head again, lift his chin, and try a second time to breathe into him. Do this to make sure his tongue is not still obstructing his airway.

If you are still unable to blow air into your child and make his chest rise, *his airway may be blocked by a foreign object.* You must try to clear the obstruction!

USE THE HEIMLICH MANEUVER for an unconscious child:

1. Kneel at your child's feet and place the heel of one hand on his abdomen, slightly *above* the navel. Re-

member to stay below the xiphoid process and the rib cage!

2. Place your other hand directly on top of the first hand and interlace your fingers. Bend your fingers back so only the heel of your hand is in place on the abdomen. (See illustration for the correct position of your hand and fingers.)

3. Press into the abdomen with a quick *upward* thrust. Make sure the thrust is *not delivered off to either side*. You may have to do several thrusts. Any one of the thrusts could dislodge the object. Careful! With a small child the thrusts should be done gently. Always adjust the force of the thrusts to the size of the child.

4. After doing several thrusts, look into your child's mouth to see if the object is now visible and can be removed. Open his mouth, depress his tongue with your thumb, and pull his jaw forward with your fin-

gers hooked under his chin. Try to remove the object only if you can see it and can get it out without pushing it farther back into the child's throat.

5. If your child is still unconscious and has not yet started breathing, *you must now try again to get air into him!*

If you are still unable to get air into your child and make his chest rise, repeat the Heimlich maneuver. Continue to check to see whether the object is visible and can be removed. Keep trying to blow air into your child and make his chest rise. *BE PERSISTENT!*

If at any time the object is expelled, you are able to remove it, or you are able to breathe into your child and make his chest rise, *his airway is cleared!* However, if he remains unconscious and does not start breathing on his own, you will have to keep breathing for him! You must also check his pulse. *If he has no pulse, you will now have to do CPR!*

YOUR CHILD IS UNCONSCIOUS!

OPEN YOUR CHILD'S AIRWAY

With your child lying flat, open his airway by lifting his chin and tilting his head back slightly. (You may have to tilt it slightly farther back than you would for an infant.)

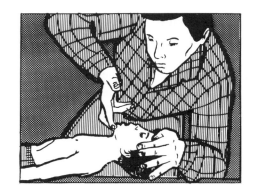

CHECK HIS BREATHING

Check to see if your child is breathing. If he is not breathing, you must *try* to breathe for him.

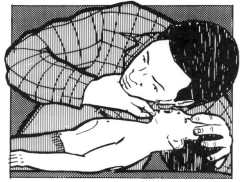

BREATHE FOR YOUR CHILD

Pinch your child's nose, put your mouth over his mouth, making an airtight seal, and blow a *slow* breath into him. If his chest does not rise, reposition his head and try again. If it still does not rise, *the airway may be obstructed by a foreign object.*

HIS AIRWAY IS OBSTRUCTED

PRESS INTO THE ABDOMEN WITH A QUICK UPWARD THRUST

Keep your hand slightly above the navel and below the xiphoid process. Make sure the thrust is *not* delivered to either side. Adjust the force you use to the size of the child. You may have to do several thrusts.

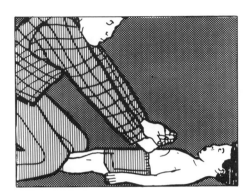

LOOK TO SEE IF THE OBJECT IS VISIBLE

Try to remove the object only if you can see it and can get it out without pushing it farther back into your child's throat.

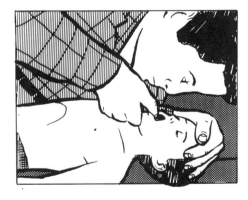

TRY TO BREATHE FOR YOUR CHILD

If your child is still unconscious and not breathing, *you must try again to get air into him.* If you still can't make his chest rise, repeat the Heimlich maneuver. Continue to check to see if the object is visible and can be removed. Keep trying to blow air into your child and make his chest rise.

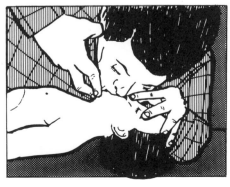

Part IV
Additional Lifesaving Information

DROWNING

Drowning is a leading cause of death for infants and young children. Children have drowned in as little as a few inches of water.

Many drownings occur when water is inhaled into the lungs, but some drownings happen when a child starts to inhale water and his throat constricts automatically, preventing him from swallowing the water. Unfortunately this also prevents the child from breathing, and he asphyxiates!

If you find your child in a near-drowning situation, you must get him out of the water immediately!* Use extreme caution, since parents themselves have drowned while attempting to save their children:

1. Before you do anything else, *open your child's airway.* Lift the chin and tilt his head back slightly. (If there is any water or debris in his mouth, turn him on his side and clear out his mouth.)

2. If your child is not breathing after you open his airway, *begin breathing for him!* Make sure his chest rises each time you blow a breath into him.

Caution: *Use the Heimlich maneuver only if you are unable to make your child's chest rise when you breathe into him.* Make sure that his head is turned to the side in case water or fluid is expelled.

3. Vomiting is very dangerous but common in a near-drowning. If your child does vomit, you must turn him to his side immediately and clean out his mouth to keep his airway and lungs clear.

4. Once you have breathed into your child and made his chest rise, *check his pulse.* (Sometimes the pulse may be harder to find because of the effects of cold water.) If you cannot find your child's pulse, *start CPR immediately!*

---

* **Caution:** If you suspect a neck or spine-injury because the child was diving, surfing, or water skiing (this is more likely to happen with older children and teenagers):

1. Move him as a unit, supporting his head, neck, and body as carefully as possible so that his head does not roll, turn, or twist in any direction. Keep his head, neck, shoulders, back, and legs in a straight line when taking him out of the water.

2. Open his airway by carefully lifting or pulling his jaw forward *without* tilting his head back. (Take a CPR course to learn this and the other lifesaving techniques necessary to save your child in a near-drowning situation.)

Very often in near-drownings, even when the child is immediately revived, serious and often fatal complications occur within hours or days afterward. For this reason, *it is extremely urgent that you get your child to a hospital after any near-drowning, even if the child is revived right away!*

Also note that children have been revived after being submerged for long periods of time, especially in cold water, so it is *always* worth starting lifesaving attempts and continuing them until emergency medical help arrives.

HOW TO GET EMERGENCY MEDICAL HELP!

When a child's life is hanging in the balance, every second counts. *YOU MUST GET HELP IMMEDIATELY!* The faster you get emergency medical help, the better your child's chances are of surviving a life-threatening situation! Yet few parents realize there are specific things they can do, even when calling for emergency medical help, to get immediate attention without wasting precious minutes. Once you realize your child is in a life-threatening situation, the first thing you must do is *YELL FOR HELP!* Keep yelling! Try to get someone to call **911** or your local Emergency Medical Services (EMS) number.

Once you begin breathing for your child or doing CPR if no one has come to your aid or summoned emergency medical help after *one minute*, you must call **911** or your local EMS number yourself.

There are two critical things to remember when telephoning for help:

1. Say exactly what's wrong: *"My baby's not breathing!"* or *"My baby has no pulse!"* These are the highest medical priorities.

2. *DON'T HANG UP!* Let the operator hang up first! In your panic you may very well forget to give the person on the phone some vital information needed to get help, such as your apartment number, your phone number—or your address!

Even while you are getting help, continue lifesaving efforts for your child! Keep breathing for him or doing CPR. Interrupt these efforts as little as possible. Continue to check for his pulse every minute or so. Continue to check to see if your child has started to breathe on his own. Continue to keep his airway open.

At BABY-LIFE, parents are taught that if they are certain their child does not have a neck or spine injury, *and if it will cause no delay in getting help*, they can take their child to the phone while continuing lifesaving efforts:*

1. For infants, use the *football carry.* You may have seen news pictures of firemen or paramedics carrying

children this way. Slide the arm that's closer to the baby's feet up under the baby's back, supporting the head and neck with your hand. Remember to keep the head tilted back only *slightly* to keep the airway open. Keep blowing breaths into the baby while you are on your way to the phone.

2. For a larger child whom you can no longer carry, use a *fireman's drag:* Kneeling behind your child's head, slip both your hands beneath his shoulders. Grasp under his arms and gently pull him along the floor, *making sure you support his head and neck with your arms.* Stop only long enough to breathe for him or to administer CPR every few feet until you reach the phone.

At BABY-LIFE, parents are advised to post important information near the phone for use in an emergency. They are told to include their telephone number and complete address, including the cross street and apartment number *(the baby-sitter may not know it), as well as these important numbers:* 911 or Emergency Medical Services, Poison Control, pediatrician, and where parents are now! *You should also include such information as your child's blood type and any special medical problems or allergies he might have.*

* **Caution:** *Never move a baby or child if you suspect a neck or spine injury* (after a bad fall, head injury, car accident, or diving mishap, for instance), unless it is absolutely necessary to move him to save his life!

Remember, if you must move him, move him as a unit, carefully supporting his head, neck, and body, so that his head does not roll, turn, or twist in any direction. Keep his head, neck, and body as straight as possible. Open his airway by carefully lifting or pulling his jaw forward *without* tilting his head back.

FOOTBALL CARRY

FIREMAN'S DRAG

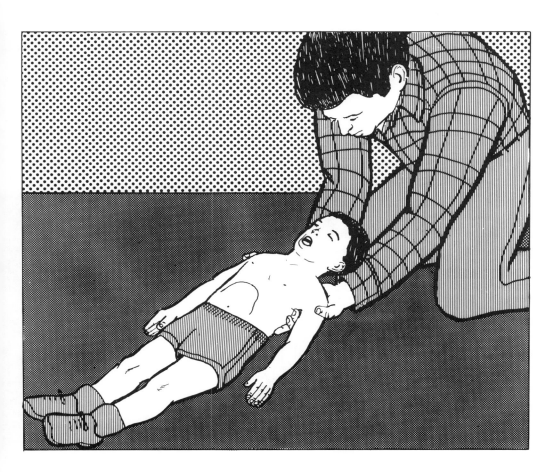

COMMON MISTAKES TO AVOID WHEN DOING LIFESAVING TECHNIQUES

Parents who take BABY-LIFE classes learn breathing for their child, CPR, and how to clear an obstructed airway. They are thoroughly drilled in these lifesaving techniques. Then they use practice dolls to demonstrate what they have learned in front of the instructor and their classmates. Most parents are nervous when they have to do this. This nervousness, coupled with their fears when they imagine having to save their own child from a life-threatening emergency, usually makes their minds go blank with panic. This might very well happen to you in real life if you were trying to save your child. Yet, because they have had so much hands-on practice, most parents in the BABY-LIFE classes are still able to perform the lifesaving techniques, *but they do make mistakes*. Since some of these mistakes are repeated so often, they are probably the very ones you would be most likely to make in a real situation—and they are the very mistakes that could prove fatal to your child!

The most common mistakes made in the BABY-LIFE classes are:

Forgetting to Open the Airway (and to Keep It Open)

Upon finding their child, parents usually remember to try to wake him up by stimulating him. But when they discover that their child is unconscious, they are often so anxious to do something to help that they immediately attempt to breathe for their child— *forgetting to open the airway!* This is why it is so important to keep in mind the ABC's of lifesaving: *AIRWAY, BREATHING, CIRCULATION!*

Remember: The first danger to an unconscious child is his own tongue. When a person is unconscious, the muscles of the throat relax and the tongue can block the airway. So the first thing you must do is get the tongue out of the way. If you attempt to breathe into your child and you have not opened the airway first, the tongue will be in the way and will prevent you from getting air into his lungs. Also, remember that sometimes just opening a child's airway will allow him to begin breathing on his own.

Breathing Too Forcefully

Parents are often so anxious to get air into their baby that they give it everything they've got! They breathe much too forcefully, or they fail to open the airway completely, or the airway is partially obstructed, which causes them to breathe with too much pressure. Breathing too forcefully can cause air to go into the stomach. This can cause your child to vomit—and vomiting is very dangerous for an unconscious child. Whatever he has thrown up can go into the lungs.

If your child vomits while he is unconscious, turn him on his side immediately and clean out his mouth to keep his airway and lungs clear. Your child may already have vomited *before* you find him. If he has, be sure to turn him on his side and clean his mouth out as best you can before you start breathing for him. If you see *any* foreign matter in your child's mouth, clean it out immediately to keep his airway and lungs clear.

Besides vomiting, another danger of getting air into the stomach is that it can cause the stomach to become so distended that it presses against the diaphragm and prevents you from getting air into the child's lungs. If this happens, you may have to *turn the child on his side* and gently try to push on his stomach to get the air out.

Caution: Pushing in on your child's stomach is very dangerous because it may also cause vomiting. *Do it only if it is absolutely necessary*—only if the stomach becomes so filled with air that you can no longer get air into your child's lungs.

Forgetting to Watch the Chest and Stomach While Breathing into Your Child

When you are blowing a breath into your child, *you must remember to watch his chest and stomach.* Parents in BABY-LIFE classes often forget to do this, but unless you watch for the chest to rise you can't be sure you are getting air into the lungs, and you will have no way of judging how forceful or how long a breath to blow. (Remember that if you see your child's stomach filling with air, it could mean either that you are blowing too hard or that his airway is not opened properly or is obstructed by a foreign object.)

Wrong Hand Placement When Doing CPR Chest Compressions

If you discovered your child had no pulse, you might be so panicked that you could very well put your hand in the wrong place when starting chest compressions. This frequently happens in BABY-LIFE classes when parents move too quickly and don't take the time to put their fingers or the heel of their hand in exactly the right place on the practice dolls to do chest compressions correctly.

Remember: If you must do CPR, take the time to find the physical landmarks on your child's body to guide you in placing your fingers or the heel of your hand. *The wrong hand placement could cause irreversible damage to your child!*

Pressing the Soft Tissue Under the Chin When Opening the Airway

When opening your child's airway by tilting the head back slightly and lifting the chin, make sure you put your fingers *only* on the bony part of the chin— *never press on the soft tissue farther back under the chin*, where you might close off the windpipe. (You may only need one finger to lift the chin of an infant, and two fingers for a child.)

QUESTIONS PARENTS ASK ABOUT LIFESAVING TECHNIQUES

Q: When I am opening the airway, how far back do I tilt my child's head?

A: In an unconscious child the muscles of the neck and throat become relaxed, allowing the tongue to block the airway. By lifting the chin and tilting the head back slightly, you move the jaw and tongue forward, clearing the airway. In a small infant, tilting the head back too far may actually pinch or close his airway, so tilt an infant's head back *only slightly*—into a level position, as if the baby were looking straight up at the ceiling. You may have to tilt it slightly farther back for an older child. You will know that you have tilted your child's head back correctly when you see his chest rise as you blow a breath into him, or if he begins breathing on his own.

Q: What happens if my baby's chest doesn't rise after I open the airway and attempt to breathe for him?

A: If your baby's chest doesn't rise, his tongue might still be obstructing his airway. (Or, with a small infant, you may have tilted his head back too far.) Try opening the airway again by lifting the chin and repositioning the head, tilting it back slightly. Then attempt to blow air into the baby. If the baby's chest still doesn't rise, or if you get air only into his stomach, your baby may have a foreign object obstructing his airway. Attempt to dislodge the object, using either back blows and chest thrusts for an infant, or the Heimlich manuever for a child.

Q: Should I clear my child's mouth out before breathing into him?

A: Clear out any foreign matter from your child's mouth if you can see it and can get it out without pushing it farther back in. If the child has vomited, or if there is fluid in his mouth, always turn him on his side to clear it out.

Q: Does having a child raise his arms when he is coughing really help, or is it an old wives' tale?

A: Thousands of parents who take BABY-LIFE classes report that when their child is *coughing effectively* to clear his throat, having him raise his arms seems to relax the child and helps him cough even more effectively. It seems to work well for adults also. However, if the child's airway is blocked by a foreign object and he *cannot cough effectively*, is having difficulty breathing, and cannot talk or cry, you must help him by using one of the lifesaving techniques for clearing an obstructed airway.

Q: Where else can I find an infant's pulse, besides his upper arm? Why can't I take the pulse in the neck, groin, or wrist, or feel directly over his heart?

A: The best place to find an infant's pulse is in the upper arm (the brachial artery). Since most babies have short, fat necks, it is difficult to find the carotid pulse in the neck. After a child is a year old and has lost much of the "baby fat" under his neck, you will be able to feel the pulse in the carotid artery. By feeling directly over the heart, you would not be feeling a true pulse. In fact, you might only be feeling irregular heart activity, which would not be circulating the blood effectively. You could look for the pulse in the wrist (radial pulse), but it may be unreliable, because the wrist is far away from the heart and the pulse may be extremely faint and difficult to feel if your child is in a weakened state, even if there is circulation. You could find either an infant's or a child's pulse in the large femoral artery in the groin (in the crease where the thigh meets the body), but you might waste time removing clothes, so it is best to take an infant's pulse in the brachial artery and a child's pulse in the carotid artery. Remember, it is important to practice taking your child's pulse.

Q: Does CPR start my baby's heart beating?

A: The purpose of CPR is not to start the heart but to keep the brain supplied with oxygen-rich blood. In *cardiac arrest* the heart has stopped pumping and can no longer circulate the blood effectively. When you do CPR you are breathing oxygen into your baby and actually pumping the oxygenated blood for the heart by doing the external chest compressions.

Q: How can I practice CPR at home?

A: *You must never practice CPR on any living thing!* It is too dangerous! You should, however, take a CPR course that includes practice on mannequins, from a certified CPR instructor. Once you have learned the techniques properly, you can review them at home using a pillow or a doll.

Q: What kind of damage can I do with CPR?

A: Even doing CPR correctly, you risk causing injury. The chest compressions have caused separated or broken ribs, damage to the sternum, and even more serious injuries. But if your child's heart has stopped beating and you do *not* do CPR, he will suffer irreversible brain damage. So if he has no pulse, *you must do CPR! It could save your child's life!* But, remember, if you do CPR *incorrectly* you might not be effec-

tive in preventing irreversible brain damage or you could cause serious injury. So take a CPR course given by a certified instructor to learn correct lifesaving skills.

Q: How fast should I do the chest compressions in CPR?

A: For an infant, chest compressions in CPR are done at the rate of about one hundred per minute. *Count:* "One, two, three, four, five." For an older child the rate is about eighty times per minute. *Count:* "One *and* two, *and* three, *and* four, *and* five." **Remember:** You must stop long enough to give a slow breath after every fifth compression.

Q: Should I take my child's clothing off before doing CPR?

A: Don't waste time removing clothes before you open the airway and attempt to breathe for your child. Remember that sometimes just opening the airway and breathing for the child is enough to save his life. However, if you find no pulse and have to do CPR, you may have to open your child's shirt or move it out of the way in order to find the right hand position to do the chest compressions.

Q: What about my fingernails when I am doing CPR?

A: If you ever have to do CPR for your infant, you will be using your fingers to do the chest compressions, and your fingernails might scratch or dig into your infant's chest. There is no way to avoid this unless, like many mothers who take BABY-LIFE classes, you keep your fingernails short. Aside from doing lifesaving techniques, short fingernails are probably a good idea for general safety around an infant or young child.

Q: What age should my baby be when I start pinching his nose while I breathe for him?

A: When your baby's mouth and nose are too large or too far apart for you to cover with your mouth (at about one year of age), you will have to cover only his mouth with your mouth, and pinch his nose when you blow a breath into him so air does not leak out.

Q: If I were doing CPR on my baby, how would I know whether to use my fingers or the heel of my hand to press down on the sternum?

A: If you were doing CPR on an infant (newborn to one year), you would use your fingers to press down on the sternum (one-half inch to an inch). Use two or three fingers, depending on the size of the baby. If you were doing CPR on a child over a year of age, you would probably be unable to press the sternum down far enough with your fingers (one inch to one and a half inches), so you could have to use the heel of your hand. However, if your child were very small at a year of age, you could try using your fingers to press the sternum down. If it didn't go down far enough, you would switch to the heel of your hand.

Q: Why can't I use the Heimlich maneuver on an infant?

A: There is still controversy about the best way to clear an infant's obstructed airway. The newest medical guidelines recommend using the Heimlich maneuver for children *over one year of age*. For infants under one year, many medical authorities are concerned about the possibility of damage to an infant's liver and other internal organs. So even though some doctors disagree, a combination of back blows and chest thrusts is the currently accepted method for clearing an infant's obstructed airway. Actually, when you are doing the back blows your baby is straddling your arm or your lap, and his midsection is pressed against you. Some experts think this abdominal pressure creates the same effect as the Heimlich maneuver.

Parents should check with their pediatrician to get his or her recommendations and should also take a CPR course to stay up to date on the methods for clearing an obstructed airway and other lifesaving techniques.

Q: How will I know I am pushing the sternum down far enough when I am doing CPR chest compressions?

A: The best way to know whether you are pushing the sternum down far enough in CPR is to have another person there who can feel for the pulse. If you are doing CPR effectively, you are actually creating a pulse that another person can feel while you are doing chest compressions. You must estimate pressing the sternum down one-half inch to one inch for an infant, and one inch to one and a half inches for a child. In BABY-LIFE classes most parents tend not to press down far enough on the practice dolls. However, when doing CPR in the panic of a real life-threatening emergency you might immediately start pressing too hard, *so be especially careful when starting to do chest compressions*. Be sure each compression is done smoothly. Do not use **poking** or jabbing movements. Spend equal time doing the compression and the release.

Q: Should I call **911** or Emergency Medical Services even if I revive my child and he seems to be okay?

A: Absolutely! If you ever have to do any lifesaving technique on your child, even if it is immediately successful your child must be seen by a doctor and checked for further complications. If you are ever concerned about your child's well-being in *any* situation, even if you only have to say "Baby, baby, are you all right?", call your pediatrician or get other medical help right away!

Part V
Prevention: Playing It Safe!

CREATING A SAFE ENVIRONMENT

The real purpose of the *BABY-LIFE* book is prevention. It is vital to know CPR, but often even CPR is not enough to save your child. The best way to keep your child safe and alive is to prevent an accident from happening in the first place!

Accidents are the leading cause of death in children, but few children have ever died from an accident while a parent was watching. Accidents usually happen when you leave your child alone—not for a half hour or fifteen minutes, or even five minutes. A moment is all it takes! You go to answer the phone or to see who is at the door. You turn your back on your child, and that's when an accident happens. This is why there is no substitute for supervision! You *must* watch your child. There are no shortcuts. Constant supervision is the best way to keep your child safe. Never forget that your child is totally dependent on you for his safety. However, since it is impossible to be with your child one hundred percent of the time, you must also create a safe environment for him.

In order to create a safe environment, you must be able to recognize life-threatening dangers and get them out of the way. Even after you have done that, your child will still have accidents—bumps and bruises are part of growing up. However, what you must prevent are the accidents that could kill your child! Drowning, choking, suffocation, strangulation, poisoning, severe burns, and terrible falls are all childhood killers. In order to prevent these tragic accidents, you have to recognize what causes them and remove the dangers from your child's environment.

All too often we learn from someone else's tragedy. There may be many hazards in your home right now that have killed other children, but you cannot always recognize these dangers by using common sense alone. Sometimes they need to be pointed out to you. However, no book can possibly show you all the dangers. Ultimately it is *your* responsibility to create a safe environment for your child. You have to develop a new awareness. Accident-proofing is a continuing process. You must anticipate your baby's changing abilities and keep up with the constant goings-on in the house. Once your awareness changes, you will be the best person to baby-proof your home. You will be able to spot a potential danger *before* it becomes a tragedy . . .

PREVENTING CHOKING

Food: Statistics indicate that one child chokes to death every five days. That's because infants and small children put *everything* in their mouths. Round, pliable objects are among the most dangerous things children put in their mouths. They can easily become stuck in a child's airway and are difficult to get out. Certain foods also fit this description, such as *hot dogs, nuts,* and *grapes,* which are among the foods children choke on most.

But even some foods that parents consider completely safe for babies are not! Bread, raisins, pieces of apple, small berries, raw carrots, cookies, and some brands of teething cracker could be dangerous and cause your child to choke! Even if your baby has front teeth, he cannot really chew food before he has his back molars (at around two years of age). His back molars are for chewing and grinding; the front teeth are used only for biting. Therefore, anything your baby has to chew before he gets his back molars could be dangerous! Bread seems harmless because it is soft, but imagine biting off a piece of bread and trying to swallow it without chewing it. You wouldn't be able to swallow it unless you chewed it a few times. What your baby does is gum the bread, which turns it into a doughy wad and makes it very easy to choke on. Certain teething crackers are hard and crisp. Once your baby has his front teeth, he will be able to bite off a chunk of the cracker, but he will not be able to chew it because he has no molars. Raisins come out of a baby the same way as they go in, so you know he is not chewing them! Clearly nature didn't intend an infant to have solid foods before he developed his back molars!

Although parents often feel pressured to give their babies solid food long before they are actually able to chew it, it is inappropriate and could be dangerous! Babies do want finger foods, but try to delay this as long as possible. Be creative. Even applesauce can be considered a finger food: The baby dips his fingers in the applesauce and licks them.

When you do decide to give your baby foods he can pick up himself, give him only foods that don't have to be chewed—foods that *melt! dissolve!* or *crumble!*

There are many foods that fit the melt, dissolve, or crumble description. Certain cereals, baby cookies, or even *very ripe* banana will melt, dissolve, or crumble when gummed. However, an apple or orange (no matter how small a piece you cut) remains solid and might very well choke a child.

Test the foods yourself before you give them to the baby. If you have to use your molars to grind or chew the food, *don't give it to your baby.* He has no molars.

European parents often chew their baby's food first. You can do this same kind of "pre-chewing" by using a food processor, blender, or a baby-food mill, or by chopping, grating, or shredding your child's food. Long cooking can also change the consistency of some foods to make them softer and more appropriate for your baby.

Once your child has his back molars, he can handle solid food, but *he is still unable to chew thoroughly.* So there are many foods that could still be dangerous! To be safe: absolutely no peanuts, no popcorn, no hard candy—and remember, no hot dogs or grapes. Pieces of meat and even lettuce, celery, carrots, and other raw vegetables, can be difficult to chew and must be shredded. Certain fruits and vegetables become stringy when chewed and can easily get caught in the throat. Peanut butter should be smooth, not chunky, and be thinly spread on a cracker or bread, *never* eaten off a finger or spooned directly out of the jar.

Almost any food can be dangerous if a child eats it while moving around. Children choke to death while crawling or running around with food in their mouths! They inhale the food instead of swallowing it. *Children should never eat while on the move.* Your child should be sitting and eating—or he should not be eating!

Toys and Small Objects: Many parents think toys or other objects that are too big to swallow are safe for their baby. They are wrong! Things have to be *too big to put in the mouth* to be competely safe. If it can fit into your baby's mouth, it can block his airway and kill him!

A couple came to a BABY-LIFE class after losing their first child. They had given him a toothpaste tube to play with. The little boy managed to get the cap off, and he choked to death on it as they watched in horror. Think about it, how many times have *you* taken the diaper-rash ointment-tube cap off and left it within your baby's reach?

This is why it is so important to keep *all* small objects out of your baby's reach. Collect everything around the house that your baby could possibly choke on: bottle and tube caps, tops of pens, paper clips, earrings, coins—anything small enough for your baby to get into his mouth—and keep it out of sight and out of reach until your child is older and stops putting things in his mouth indiscriminately.

Your baby is also very likely to put his toys in his mouth. One of the most common toys found in homes where BABY-LIFE classes are taught is a small plastic Little People toy. Parents feel the toy is safe because it is too big for the baby to swallow. But if a baby or young child can put any toy all the way into his mouth, it can get caught in his throat and stop him from breathing! To be absolutely safe, *toys must be as big as your child's fist—too big to fit into the mouth!* To help prevent your child from choking, remember:

• Check toys for loose parts, such as little wheels from cars, a button from a doll's dress, the eye of a stuffed animal. All of these can choke your child.

• Keep rubber balloons away from babies and young children. If a child puts a deflated balloon or a piece of broken balloon in his mouth, the rubber gets very slippery, and this makes it very easy for the balloon to slide to the back of the throat, block his airway, and prevent him from breathing. According to the Consumer Product Safety Commission, more children have choked on balloons than on any other toy!

• Test all buttons on dolls' clothing and on your child's clothing. Babies can use their front teeth to bite off buttons.

• Make sure that rubber squeeze toys are too big to fit in the mouth when compressed.

• Use foam-rubber toys with care. It is true that a child won't bump or bruise himself on a foam toy, but he could bite off a piece of the foam and choke on it. Inspect foam toys periodically, and for small babies, use them only when supervised.

- Check pacifiers and nipples frequently. They get worn and come apart. Also, never leave them in the crib overnight! Be sure the pacifier is designed so that the baby cannot possibly get it completely into his mouth.

- Take all toys out of the baby's crib at night, or when he is napping.

- Never use Styrofoam as a child's toy. It is extremely dangerous! Don't use styrofoam cups. It is very easy for a child to bite off a piece of the Styrofoam and choke on it. Get all Styrofoam packing material out of the house immediately. Toys often come packaged in it.

- Do not rely *only* on a "no-choke tube," a device used to measure whether a toy is too big to choke on. There are reports of children's choking on toys that would have passed the "no-choke tube" test. The best way to keep an infant or young child safe from choking on a toy or object is to keep *all* small objects out of reach, and *make sure all toys are too big to fit into his mouth!*

PREVENTING SUFFOCATION

Suffocation is a major cause of death for babies, especially newborns. Some deaths attributed to sudden infant death syndrome have later been found to be caused by suffocation. Remember, there are many ways you can help keep your child safe from suffocating:

- Use lightweight thermal blankets with an open waffle weave for infants. Heavier blankets prevent babies from turning freely and could cause suffocation.

- Never leave heavy blankets or clothing draped over a crib railing where they could accidentally fall into the crib, cover the baby's face, and suffocate him.

- Don't use pillows in the baby's crib.

- Don't put a cloth diaper under your baby's face in his crib to catch drooling. (This old "nanny custom" could cause babies to suffocate.)

- Keep disposable diapers out of your baby's reach. The plastic covering could suffocate a baby, and the little closing tab could choke him.

- Never use plastic coverings of any kind on the crib mattress.

- Never leave infants alone on beds, water beds, or upholstered furniture. Infants have suffocated after being wedged between the mattress and wall or headboard on beds, and even between the cushions of sofas.

Plastic bags: Everyone knows about the dangers of plastic bags—and yet many babies still suffocate because of them!

One little girl crawled into her daddy's closet and pulled the thin plastic dry-cleaning bag off his suit. She was found suffocated moments later.

Thin, filmy, transparent plastic can be extremely dangerous and can suffocate a child. Babies are attracted to it because it is crinkly. They seek it out and often put it over their faces or heads. Even having it in closets and drawers is not safe, so get any thin, filmy plastic out of the house! Tie it in knots, put it in the trash can, and make sure your child can't possibly fish it out. Also, plastic bags and plastic wrap used in the kitchen could be dangerous and should be kept well out of baby's reach.

PREVENTING STRANGULATION

Strangulation is another serious danger for small children. An infant or small child has a delicate neck. At birth a baby has no muscle development in his neck, he has only soft tissue. It doesn't take much pressure to cut off circulation to the brain.

One baby-sitter unthinkingly gave a baby a toy telephone to play with in his crib. The baby managed to get the cord on the phone around his neck. When his parents came home later, they went to check on the baby and found him strangled in his crib.

Another child, just learning to crawl, got his head caught in the rungs of a rocking chair in his room. Apparently he turned his head sideways, slipped it between the rungs to get it in, and then couldn't get himself out. He panicked, yanked as hard as he could, and wedged himself in more tightly. Even though his mother was in the next room, he strangled to death. Strangulation dangers are sometimes difficult to spot unless they are pointed out to you:

• Remove all cords, play gyms, strings, or bars suspended across or around the crib or playpen well before the baby is able to sit up or push himself up. This usually happens around five months, but watch your baby closely. Some babies are able to push themselves up or sit up sooner than others.

• Never tie toys, rattles, or pacifiers to a crib railing, playpen, or stroller. The baby could strangle on the cord.

• Never put a baby's pacifier on a string around his neck.

• Cut all strings on pull toys to five inches or less, so they cannot get wrapped around a baby's neck.

• Cut cords from toy telephones.

• Don't leave the high chair, crib, or playpen near venetian blind or telephone cords. Tack up venetian blind cords well out of baby's reach. Children have strangled on them! If the kitchen or other wall phone has a long cord, wrap it around the phone or tack it to the wall.

• Take the strings out of hooded sweatshirts.

• Don't leave scarves, ties, or any other clothing lying around that a baby can wrap around his neck.

PREVENTING BURNS

A couple was busily preparing for their child's first birthday party. They left the little boy alone in the kitchen for just a few moments. They didn't think he could get into any trouble because he hadn't learned to climb yet.

Although his parents didn't know it, this little boy *had* learned how to push a kitchen chair in front of him and use it to climb to places he couldn't reach. He managed to get the chair against the stove. There were cookies on a shelf over the stove, and that's where he was headed. As he reached to pull himself up, he grabbed a pot of boiling water, pulled it down, and scalded himself to death!

A tragedy like this is one of the reasons BABY-LIFE was started.

Kitchen Burns: The kitchen is one of the most dangerous rooms in the house! A baby can get scalded, poisoned, cut, and more, in the kitchen. *Never, ever leave your baby in the kitchen unsupervised!* Even if you are there with him, the kitchen can be a risky place for your baby. To help prevent kitchen burns, remember:

• Never let the baby crawl around the kitchen while you are cooking. To prevent scalds or hot-food spills, always put him in his high chair or playpen.

• Always use the back burners. Even older children can have accidents with front burners or hot food on the stove.

• Keep hot liquids—soups, coffee— away from the edges of tables and countertops. Don't use tablecloths.

• Never drink coffee, tea, or any other hot liquid with a baby in your lap.

• Never store treats or goodies over the stove.

• Always test baby's formula or milk after heating it. Be especially careful if you are using a microwave. Babies can suffer second- and third-degree burns of the mouth and throat from milk that is too hot—and this is most likely to happen in a microwave. Containers of food or liquids heated in a microwave often feel cool to the touch, but their contents can be hot enough to scald.

Electrical Burns: Ordinary household current is powerful enough to cause severe burns. Electricity not only burns the surface of the skin, but it can also do terrible internal damage to tissues and nerves as the electrical current travels through the body. Many infants have been left disfigured by electrical burns of the mouth and lips. To help lessen the risk of electrical burns to your child:

• Unplug electric appliances when you are not using them: toasters, toaster ovens, microwaves, can openers, blenders, food processors, mixers, hair dryers—anything that could accidentally be turned on or conduct electricity even when it is switched off.

• Never let a child play behind the TV. If it works on remote control, it can store electricity even when it is off.

• Keep all electrical outlets covered when there is nothing plugged into them. Use outlet covers that your child cannot remove. Children tend to stick things in electrical outlets, or even put their mouths over them.

• Make sure your child cannot pull plugs from outlets. Either move something in front of the outlet or buy a device that prevents him from pulling the plug out.

• Unplug extension cords from the wall outlet when they are not in use. If you must leave an extension cord plugged in, use one of the newer safety extension cords, or tape the plugs together with electrical tape to keep your baby from putting the live end in his mouth. Babies also suffer burns of the mouth from biting on electrical wires, so keep all wires out of reach!

Fire Safety: In case of fire, grab the baby and get out immediately! Don't waste time fighting a blaze or calling the fire department from your house. Even if you only smell smoke, leave! *A baby can die within minutes from smoke inhalation!* To help prevent fire tragedies, remember:

• Be sure that everyone in the family, including the care-giver, knows the escape plan in case of fire!

• When leaving a smoke-filled room, keep children and yourself as low to the ground as possible. This could be a lifesaver!

• If you live in an apartment and there is a fire in the building, test the door before leaving to make sure it is not hot and that the hallway is not filled with smoke.

• Smoke detectors near children's rooms—and throughout the house—are a must!

• Keep a fire extinguisher (out of the child's reach) and some baking soda near your stove to use if there is a *small* kitchen fire that can be put out quickly. If the fire is not extinguishable immediately, get everyone out of the house.

• Many babies have started fatal fires by rubbing cigarette lighters on the carpet or on the floor. Keep all matches and cigarette lighters well out of sight and out of reach, where babies and young children can't possibly get to them. (Over one hundred children under five die each year in fires caused by cigarette lighters.)

PREVENTING POISONING

Accidental poisonings are one of the leading pediatric emergencies. Approximately eighty percent of all poison victims are children, and as many as ninety percent of these are children under five years old. Infants and young children will put anything in their mouths—no matter how bad it tastes!

Never rely *only* on your ability to stop your child before he swallows a poison. This is a mistake. A baby is quick, and whatever he gets into his hand can go into his mouth before you can do anything to stop it.

A father doing the laundry with his son nearby learned this tragic lesson. As he turned to check the dryer, his little boy drank almost half a bottle of Clorox! The father had only turned away for a moment. He should have put the cap on the bottle and moved it to a higher shelf, *out of reach!*

Out of sight! Out of reach! and *Locked up!* are the keys to poison-proofing your home.

Cleansers/Household Poisons:

Household cleansers are one of the most common sources of poisons for babies and young children. All household cleaning products must be kept up high and locked up. Many of them are extremely toxic and dangerous—bleaches, ammonia, oven cleaners, pine-oil cleaners, dishwasher detergent, furniture polish. Other toxic products, such as drain openers, which contain lye, could actually disfigure or blind a child! Also be aware that mixing household cleansers such as ammonia and bleach can create toxic fumes.

Keeping toxic cleansers in cabinets under the kitchen or bathroom sink, even with a safety latch on the cabinet door, is not safe. Children frequently learn to manipulate and open these safety latches, or you may be distracted and forget to close the cabinet door securely. That's when your child could seize the opportunity to drink the lemon-scented furniture polish! To help prevent household poisonings, remember:

• If the phone or doorbell rings while you are using a poisonous substance, take the child with you or get the poison out of sight, out of reach, and locked up.

- Never turn your back on a child when there is a poisonous substance nearby.

- Put tops back on bottles and cans as soon as you are finished using them.

- Never store poisons near food.

- Never put anything that is not edible in a food or drink container. People frequently use empty soda bottles or milk containers to store gasoline, solvents, or other dangerous poisons. Keep all toxic substances in their original containers, clearly marked.

- Just one capful of electric dishwasher detergent can badly burn a child's mouth and throat.

- Boric acid and pesticides can be extremely toxic. Don't sprinkle them on the floor where the baby crawls.

- Antifreeze in even the smallest amount is lethal!

- Swallowing small disc batteries has become a widespread cause of injury for children. The chemical in-side the battery can leak and burn the esophagus and stomach.

Medicines: Medicines are one of the most frequent and most lethal sources of childhood poisonings. Prescription drugs are particularly dangerous, as are aspirin, aspirin substitutes (which can be as toxic as aspirin), mentholated chest rubs, over-the-counter eye drops, after-shave, or anything else found in the medicine cabinet! Remember:

- Keep all medicines and drugs in a locked cabinet.

- Never call medicines candy.

- Avoid taking medicines in front of your children. Young children like to imitate everything their parents do.

- Don't forget that child-resistant caps are not always childproof! They slow children down but don't necessarily keep them from getting the caps off.

Easily Overlooked Poisons: Babies love to explore Mommy's pocketbook, but this is often overlooked as a source of poisons. Yet it might contain things as diverse—and deadly—as perfume, nasal spray, cold-sore medicine, tranquilizers, medications, or worse. Keep your pocketbook in a drawer or closet that your child cannot get into. Also, be especially careful when visiting, or when visitors come to your house. Grandmother, for instance, might have pills for a heart condition in her purse. Remember, there are many other unexpected toxic substances that could easily poison a baby or small child:

- *Vitamin pills:* A handful of iron supplements can be fatal to a child.

- *Table salt:* One teaspoon can kill a baby.

- *Cigarettes and tobacco:* Nicotine is a poison. Babies have become seriously ill from chewing on discarded cigarette butts. One stick of nicotine-based chewing gum could cause convulsions in your child.

- *Alcohol:* Babies have died from ingesting alcohol (left over from a party for instance). Keep the liquor cabinet securely locked!

- *Mouthwash:* Children often drink mouthwash after watching their parents use it. It contains enough alcohol to kill a child if taken in large enough amounts.

- *Nutmeg:* In large quantities nutmeg can cause convulsions and hallucinations!

- *Household plants:* These are a common source of childhood poisonings. Call your local Poison Control Center and get a list of poisonous plants. Then, check all your plants. Make sure that you can identify those you have and that none of them is toxic. If you are not sure about a particular plant, take a leafy branch to your local nursery or plant store.

Note: If you have any doubts about the toxicity of *any* substance, call your local Poison Control Center and find out whether it is poisonous. The number should be posted next to your telephone!

PREVENTING FALLS

Falling is a frequent household accident. An infant falling from a changing table, down a flight of stairs, or even off a bed can suffer a crippling—or even fatal—injury. Never turn your back on an infant, or leave him alone on a bed, changing table, or any high place—even for a moment! It is very common to put a baby in the middle of the bed or on the sofa. You think he can't roll over, you turn to do something, and that's when he suddenly learns to roll over and falls off the bed.

A mother put her infant on the kitchen counter in an infant seat while she was doing the dishes, so the baby could see her. The child shifted his weight, tipped the infant seat off the counter, and landed on the kitchen floor, hitting his head and suffering a brain-damaging injury. To prevent tragic falls like this from happening, remember:

• The only safe place for a baby in an infant seat is on the floor! You never know when your baby will be able to shift his weight and send himself and the seat crashing to the floor. Also, always remember to use the safety strap when your baby is in the infant seat.

• Falls from cribs and changing tables are so universal, many parents think they are a normal part of growing up and don't realize how dangerous they can be. When your child is in his crib with the mattress fully lowered, the crib railing should come at least three quarters of the way up his body, or to his mid-chest. If it doesn't, your child has outgrown his crib, and he can easily tumble out, headfirst. Height—not age—determines when your baby has outgrown his crib.

• Crawling babies and toddlers are especially vulnerable to falling down stairs. Use gates at both the top and the bottom of the stairs. Use an approved safety gate, not the old-style accordion gates with large diamond cutouts or V-shaped openings that could entrap your child. Use a sturdy gate that can be securely fastened to the wall or the banister on either side. Even with a safety gate, keep your baby away from the top of the stairs.

- Keep all furniture, such as beds, sofas, chairs, or anything else a baby could climb on, away from windows.
- Window guards, in most cities, are mandated by law in homes with young children. However, to be really safe, all windows within a small child's reach should be kept securely closed and locked! Children most often fall out of open windows; however, they have even fallen through screened windows as well.

BATHROOM HAZARDS

The bathroom is another of the most dangerous rooms in the house. You must use one hundred percent supervision—one hundred percent of the time—when you are bathing your baby! This means your child must be in your sight at all times. For an infant, *your hand must be on him at all times*. A baby can drown in a couple of inches of water, just enough to cover his nose and mouth. Even the toilet bowl can be dangerous! To help keep your child safe in the bathroom, remember:

- Never, ever turn your back on a baby or young child in the bathtub—or around any water—not even for a moment!

- Babies have drowned while using tub rings. Remember, your hand must be on a baby at all times when he is in the bath.

- Never allow a baby or young child in the bathroom unsupervised. If he can reach the bathroom doorknob, use a hook and eye that only you can reach to keep the door securely closed from the outside.

- Use a non-skid mat in the tub, and on the bathroom floor.

- Put a towel, sponge, or specially designed foam toy over the faucet so your child won't bang his head on it.

- Keep the hot-water temperature at 120° F. The hot water in many homes is hotter than this. Water set at 135° F. could give a child a serious burn in seconds.

- Turn the hot water off first, and the cold water off last, so your child won't scald himself.

- Remember to keep all medications, mouthwash, bathroom cleansers, and other toxic substances out of sight, out of reach, and locked up if possible.

- Take all electrical appliances out of the bathroom—especially the hair dryer! A baby was killed when a hair dryer that was only plugged in, not turned on, was accidentally dropped in his bath.

FURNITURE HAZARDS

Your baby could easily be crushed by the chest of drawers in his room! Babies can pull open the bottom drawer and climb on it, shifting the center of gravity, which causes the entire chest to topple over on them. Test the furniture in your child's room: Pull open the bottom drawer and notice how easy it is to tip over the chest.

A simple hook and eye can be used to anchor furniture such as a chest of drawers or a bookcase to the wall and will prevent baby from pulling it down on top of himself. Babies love to reach up and pull down. Take these precautions to help keep your child safe around furniture:

- Don't keep anything heavy on shelves or tabletops within a child's reach. A child was crushed to death when she pulled a TV down off a table.

- The spaces between chair rungs and banister railings should be narrow enough so a child cannot put his head or body through them.

- Reclining chairs with footrests that open up create a dangerous space in which a child can become entrapped. A little girl was left brain-dead when her neck became entrapped in the space between the reclining chair and the footrest, and she was unable to breathe.

- Cover hard-edged furniture—glass, marble, or Formica—with heavy padded blankets (movers' quilts work well), or store the furniture away until your child is older. It is not only the pointed corners on furniture that are dangerous; any hard protruding edge can crack a child's skull or cause a severe gash if he falls against it.

- Babies have gone head- or hand-first through glass doors, killing or disfiguring themselves. To prevent this, make sure all glass doors and glass-fronted furniture are made of safety glass. Use decals or brightly colored tape at the baby's eye level, or put something in front of the glass doors to keep children from going through them.

SWIMMING POOL HAZARDS

Many if not most childhood drownings happen in backyard swimming pools. Yet few parents ever realize just how hazardous a pool can be, or take enough precautions to make sure their child is safe around the pool. No matter how many precautions you take, however, the *only* way to keep your child truly safe around water is *not to take your eyes off him*, not even for a second! To help prevent swimming pool tragedies:

- The pool itself, *not* just the property, must have a fence around it, with a self-closing gate that has a self-locking mechanism. Many states require this by law.

- Be sure to empty wading pools immediately after each use, and deflate them or turn them over to keep rainwater from collecting in them.

- Bicycles, tricycles, and other play equipment should never be used around a swimming pool. *The swimming pool is not a play area!*

- Don't depend *solely* on swim rings, water wings, or foam floaters. These flotation devices do not drownproof your child! Young children can still go face-down in the water, or slip out of a swim ring entirely.

Remember: Children have drowned in two or three inches of water! Constant and close supervision is the *only* way to keep a child safe around water of any kind!

BABY EQUIPMENT

Car Seats: Car seats have saved more children's lives than any other safety device. You must use them *every* time your baby is in the car. In many states it is the law that children must use car seats until they are at least four years old.

There is no way you can safely hold a baby on your lap—even at five or ten miles per hour (the speed you might be going just pulling out of the driveway or going around the corner to the store). An accident that would leave you unharmed could kill or maim your baby!

The middle of the backseat is the safest place to keep the car seat. An infant must face the back of the car until he can sit up by himself or until he weighs twenty pounds. When your baby outgrows the car seat, use a booster seat until he is old enough to use the car seat belts and shoulder straps (at least four years of age). *Improper use of a car seat can be almost as dangerous as not using it at all*, so follow manufacturers' instructions closely.

Cribs: Make sure the railings on the crib are no more than two and three-eighths inches (about three fingers' width) apart to prevent the baby's head or body from slipping through. When a baby can slip his body through the railings on a crib, his head, being larger, gets caught in the railings, causing strangulation. The mattress must fit snugly so the baby's head cannot get wedged between the mattress and crib. Never use cribs with corner posts, knobs, or other decorative extensions that stick up even a little bit at the end of the crib and could snag baby's clothing. A little girl was strangled when her clothing was caught on a corner post at the foot of her crib! Cribs with foot or headboard cutouts or designs that could allow a baby's neck to become entrapped in the opening are also dangerous! Be sure there are no cords, strings, play gyms, toys, or bars hanging across or around the crib once your baby is able to push himself up.

High Chairs, Carriages, and Strollers: You must use a safety strap each and every time your baby is in his high chair, carriage, or stroller. Even the most expensive models are capable of tipping over! Use a three-way strap whenever possible—one that comes up through the baby's crotch.

Never push a stroller into the street without first checking to see if traffic is coming. Remember that the stroller sticks out in front of you by at least three feet!

Playpens: Playpens are a relatively safe place to leave the baby, but be sure the one you choose conforms to the latest safety standards. Never use a mesh-sided playpen with one side partially lowered. Babies have suffocated when caught between the mesh and the side of the mattress. Also, mesh netting should be a small weave—smaller than the buttons on baby's clothing.

A playpen should always be kept where you can see it, in a safe area where the baby can't reach anything dangerous. You should also inspect playpen teething railings frequently. A baby can bite through the vinyl-covered foam railings and choke on pieces of the foam.

Toy Chests: Toy chests with lids have caused many accidents that have left children brain-damaged.

Make sure you use a toy chest that has a spring-loaded hinge, which automatically keeps the top open at any point, and be sure there are air holes or spaces for ventilation. Or better yet, take the lid off entirely. It's also a good idea to buy spring-loaded hinges for other furniture with lids, such as piano benches or blanket chests. If this is not possible, make sure the child can't open them.

Portable Table Seats: Portable table seats should be used only while you are sitting next to your child. A portable seat is not a substitute for a high chair. Avoid leaving a kitchen chair under the portable table seat when your child is sitting in it. If he pushes his feet against the chair he can cause the seat to release from the edge of the table.

Baby Walkers: There is considerable controversy about the use of baby walkers. Many doctors don't recommend them at all, so before using one, check with your own pediatrician. Since there have been many accidents with baby walkers, if you do use them use them only when the baby is closely supervised. Use only on smooth-surfaced floors, and remove throw rugs. Be especially careful of baby walkers around stairs.

There is also controversy about the use of baby jumpers, so check with your pediatrician before using them.

Automatic Swings: Automatic swings can be used safely and babies seem to enjoy them, but, like other infant play equipment, they should be used only when the baby is closely supervised.

Part VI
First Aid

THE BASICS OF FIRST AID

BABY-LIFE parents frequently express the fear that they will panic if their child needs first aid, and will not know what to do first.

You may panic, but if you do, you can control it. The key is to slow down. Speed or rushing can actually create panic, but if you move slowly you will feel more in control. This is why, in any first-aid emergency, the first thing you must do is take a *five- or ten-second survey*. This will allow you to see what has happened, and what needs to be done:

- Look to see what has caused the injury. *Is any danger still present?*

- Is your child *unconscious?* If so, remember the most important rule in first aid: Take care of the *AIRWAY, BREATHING, CIRCULATION* first.

- If your child is *conscious*, check his behavior. Is he alert?

- If your child is old enough, ask him what happened and let him show you where he is hurt.

These initial five or ten seconds will also calm you, and will prevent you from doing anything in haste that could further injure your child.

For example, if your baby has fallen and he is crying loudly, you know two things: He is breathing and he is alert. He is probably not in an immediately life-threatening situation.

But if he is lying at the foot of the stairs after a bad fall and he is not moving or making any noise, he might have a broken neck or a spine injury, and the worst thing you could possibly do is rush over and pick him up!

Remember, never move a child (or anyone) if you suspect a neck or spine injury, unless doing so is absolutely necessary to save his life! If you do have to move your child for safety reasons, or to take care of the *AIRWAY, BREATHING,* and *CIRCULATION,* remember to move him as a unit, supporting his head, neck, and body as carefully as possible so that his head does not roll, turn, or twist in any direction. Keep his head, neck, and body in a straight line. Open his airway by carefully lifting or pulling his jaw forward *without* tilting his head back.

After you've taken care of the *AIRWAY, BREATHING, CIRCULATION,* the next most important thing you must do is *stop any serious bleeding with direct pressure.* This is especially important with infants and young children. What seems like a small blood loss for an adult can cause shock or even death in a child.

It is usually best not to give your child anything to eat or drink right after a very serious injury, because it could cause complications later.

In any first-aid emergency you must get medical help immediately! If possible, get someone else to call for help while you stay with your child. *Offering your child calm reassurance can be as important as any treatment you give.*

Note: To learn first aid and lifesaving techniques properly, take a first-aid course given by a certified instructor.

BLEEDING

Next to not breathing, bleeding can be the most serious medical emergency! Little babies don't have very much blood to begin with, so a loss of blood that might be insignificant in an adult can be extremely serious in a small child.

You must stop any bleeding *immediately!* Most bleeding can be stopped with *direct pressure:*

- Use a clean compress such as a sterile gauze pad, a towel, a sanitary napkin, a folded handkerchief, or any clean, thick pad of cloth. If you have nothing else, you can use your hand.

- Apply the compress directly to the wound. Press as hard as you can and hold it there.

- If the bleeding is severe and the bandage soaks through, *do not remove it!* Apply more compresses on top and continue the direct pressure more firmly. (When the bleeding stops, do not remove the compress. Wrap a bandage over the compress to secure it on the wound.)

Elevation can also help slow bleeding from an arm or leg. Continue direct pressure and elevate the limb above the heart—only if you are sure there is no fracture, and if it doesn't cause pain.

If direct pressure and elevation alone do not stop the bleeding in the arm or leg, use *pressure points* (while continuing direct pressure and elevation):

- *To help stop bleeding in the arm:* Use the brachial artery on the inside of the upper arm, between the elbow and the armpit. While continuing to use elevation and direct pressure on the wound with one hand, use your other hand to grasp the upper arm, with your thumb on the outer part of the arm and your fingers flat and straight on the inside part of the arm. Firmly press the inside of the upper arm against the bone.

- *To help stop bleeding in the leg:* Use the femoral artery in the crease of the groin, where the thigh meets the body. With the child lying down, and while continuing to use elevation and direct pressure on the wound with one hand, use the heel of the other hand to press on the pressure point. Push hard with the heel of your hand on the crease.

Tourniquets are rarely needed. They can be dangerous because they cut off all blood supply to the tissue and should be used only as a last resort!

Note: For a finger or a fingertip that is accidentally cut off, stop the bleeding with direct pressure, and *save the remaining piece.* Wrap it in plastic, if possible. Keep it cool in ice water, but protect it from direct contact with ice. Get emergency medical help!

For any deep or serious wound, *get emergency medical help immediately!* And even for seemingly minor cuts, and especially puncture wounds, get medical advice right way, since your child may need a tetanus shot or stitches. The biggest danger with minor cuts and scrapes is infection, so be sure to wash in and around the wound gently with soap and water, and rinse thoroughly. Blot dry, and then cover with a sterile bandage.

Nosebleeds: Other than minor cuts and scrapes, nosebleeds may happen to your child more than anything else in his young years. However, they are simple to treat:

• Keep your child sitting upright or leaning slightly forward.

• Keep his head level. Do not tilt it back.

• Pinch the nose closed just below the bridge, and keep it closed as long as necessary to stop the bleeding.

• If the nosebleed lasts longer than a few minutes, call your pediatrician.

SHOCK

After any accident, you must always give first aid and treat any injury immediately. But when the injury is serious, you must also anticipate the possibility of shock.

In children, shock can result not only from blood loss in the case of a serious injury, but from fluid loss from severe burns, or even from prolonged illness, vomiting, or diarrhea.

Some of the signs and symptoms of shock are pale, cold, clammy skin, rapid pulse, nausea, and severe thirst. Your child might also appear restless, frightened, and apprehensive.

When your child is in a state of shock, his vital organs are not receiving enough oxygen through the blood, and irreversible tissue damage can occur. This is why it is vitally important in the event of any serious injury or illness to *get emergency medical help as quickly as possible!*

While you are waiting for help to arrive, it is best to keep your child lying down:

• If your child is *unconscious*, breathing, and has no neck or spine injury,

keep him on his side in case he vomits, and to keep his tongue from blocking his airway.

• If your child is *conscious*, with no neck or spine injury, elevate his feet (about ten to twelve inches), unless it causes pain or he has a fractured leg.

• If your child has a severe head injury, his head should be level or higher, not lower, than the rest of his body.

• If your child is conscious and has difficulty breathing, you may sit him up, or let him assume a position where he finds it easiest to breathe, provided he has no neck or spine injury.

• Cover your child just enough to maintain his body temperature and prevent him from becoming chilled. (Do not overheat him.)

Remember: Treat any serious injury first, and don't forget that reassuring your child and keeping him comfortable and as free from pain as possible can also help prevent shock.

BURNS

The first step in treating *any* burn is to *stop the burning!* If your child's clothes are on fire, or smoldering, snuff out the flames, smother them. Wrap him in a blanket, coat, or whatever is at hand, or even roll him on the floor. With a chemical burn, you must wash off the chemicals as quickly as possible. For an electrical burn, you have to break the connection or cut off the power supply.

Next, cool the burn and treat it according to how serious it is:

First-Degree Burns: A child can get
a *first-degree burn* from touching something too hot. He pulls his fingers away immediately, and they may be slightly red and feel painful. Getting a mild sunburn or spilling hot liquids on himself could also give a child a first-degree burn.

There are no blisters or swelling in a first-degree burn, just reddened skin and pain. First-degree burns have to be *cooled off immediately:*

• Use cold (not ice) water to cool the burn. Either immerse the burn or gently run cold water on it until the pain subsides, or until the child stops crying. (If you can't get cold water directly on the burn, use compresses that have been wrung out in cold water.)

• Never use ice directly on a burn. It can damage the tissue.

• Never use butter or grease on a burn. It inhibits healing and could cause infection.

Second-Degree Burns: These burns
are more serious and very often occur from scalding, flash burns (for instance, when an oven momentarily flares up while being lit), or severe sunburn.

Second-degree burns are deeper, the skin is red or mottled, and there is usually swelling or blistering. Don't break the blisters—they protect against infection. Second-degree burns must be *cooled off immediately:*

• Cool second-degree burns with cold water or compresses until the pain eases. Gently blot dry and apply a sterile gauze dressing.

• If your child is scalded, remove his wet clothing if it comes off easily and is not stuck to the skin, and cool the burn. If the clothing doesn't come off easily, don't waste time!

Saturate the clothes with cold running water to cool the burn immediately.

Caution: First- or second-degree burns should be considered very serious if they cover more than just a small area of a child's body. If a *large area* of a child's body has been burned, cover him lightly with a clean dry sheet and get emergency medical help immediately. *Since cold can worsen a possible shock reaction, do not immerse the child's entire body in a tub of cold water or do anything else that might chill him.* Children who are badly burned very often die from shock.

Even after minor burns consult your pediatrician, because with babies and young children there is always a danger of scarring, infection, or other complications.

Third-Degree Burns: These burn through all layers of the skin. The skin might be white and waxy, or dark and charred-looking. (It is sometimes hard to distinguish between a second- and a third-degree burn.)

Third-degree burns can be caused by clothing on fire, electricity, or immersion in scalding water. With any third-degree burn, infection, shock, or other complications are the biggest threats. If your child suffers a third-degree burn:

- Stop the burning first!

- Never try to remove charred clothing stuck to the burned skin.

- Do not apply ice directly or immerse your child's entire body in a tub of cold water to cool a third-degree burn. This can intensify a shock reaction and can also increase the risk of infection.

- Never apply any ointments or salves. They will only have to be scraped off later.

- Cover your child lightly with a clean sheet or a sterile dressing.

- Get emergency medical help immediately! The possibility of shock with all severe burns is great, especially in babies and young children. If you do not expect medical help to reach you within an hour, and your child is conscious, alert, and not vomiting, let him sip a commercially prepared electrolyte replacement drink, or dissolve one teaspoon of salt and one-half teaspoon of baking soda in a quart of tepid water and let your child sip it to help prevent dehydration and shock. Give only one ounce to an infant, and two ounces to a child.

Burns of the Hands, Feet, Face, and Genitals:
These burns should always be considered serious and should be seen immediately by a doctor to avoid later complications such as scar tissue:

- A child with face burns should be kept sitting up. Watch for any breathing difficulty.

- Severely burned hands should be kept above the level of the heart, and burned feet or legs should be elevated.

- A well-insulated, dry cold pack can be applied very gently to the face, hands, feet, or genitals to alleviate pain.

Smoke Inhalation:
Smoke can severely burn a child's lungs or throat and later cause swelling that could hinder his breathing. This is why, with smoke inhalation, you must get emergency medical help, even if your child *seems* all right!

Chemical Burns:
Chemical burns can be either alkali or acid. Common acids around the house are toilet-bowl cleansers and rust removers. Common alkalis you might have in your home are lye and drain cleaners, strong laundry and dishwasher detergents, and other cleaning solutions such as ammonia.

If a strong chemical gets on your child's skin, wash it off immediately! All chemical burns, no matter how small, should be flooded with water. Alkaline burns (especially of the eye) must be flushed with water for a longer time than acid burns, since even after the pain stops, tissue damage can continue:

- Flood the burned area for at least five minutes, even if it means putting your child in the shower.

Caution: If your child has been chemically burned, *never* put him in a tub of water or immerse the body part, because it will spread the chemical and cause a much more serious burn.

- Remove clothing from all chemical burns.

- Never scrub or use soap on a chemical burn.

• Apply a dry, sterile gauze dressing after you have washed off the chemical.

• If the chemical is in the eye, flush it out thoroughly, being careful not to wash the chemical into the other eye. Continue to flush with water for at least fifteen minutes, even after the pain has stopped, to prevent further damage to the underlying eye tissue.

• Call **911** or your EMS number to get emergency medical help, and call the Poison Control Center to find out if there is anything else you can do.

Electrical Burns: Your child can suffer a burn from electricity as well as from heat! With any electric shock the first thing you must do is remove the source of electricity. Turn off the power or pull the plug. Or get the child away from the source of electricity. Stand on a *dry surface* and use a *nonconductive* material such as a thick cloth towel looped around him, or a wooden chair or a broom handle to knock him away. Do not grab your child's body, or you will get a shock too!

If your child is unconscious, the next thing you must take care of is the *AIR-WAY, BREATHING, CIRCULATION.* Make sure your child has an open airway, is breathing, and has a pulse. If he isn't breathing, breathe for him; if he has no pulse, begin CPR.

If he is breathing and has a pulse, check for burn marks. With an electrical burn there will be marks where the electricity entered *and* where it exited. Cover the burn sites with a dry, clean dressing, treat for shock, and get emergency medical help immediately! Since the greatest damage from electrical burns is done internally, they can be far more serious than they first appear, *so any electrical burn should always be seen immediately by a doctor!*

Sunburn: Babies and young children have tender skin, and they burn easily. Sunburn can be extremely dangerous to babies, especially if it covers more than just a small area.

For small sunburned areas, cool the skin with water or cold compresses. If the burn is mild and there are no blisters, apply soothing lotion. Lightly cover a large sunburned area with a clean, dry sheet, make sure your child is as comfortable as possible, and *call your pediatrician at once!*

Keep babies and small children out of direct sun, especially during peak hours.

POISONING

You might not actually see your child take poison, but you may suspect that he has if:

- You find him with an open container of a poisonous substance.

- He becomes suddenly ill and shows signs of nausea, vomiting, lethargy, or unusual behavior.

- He has severe abdominal pains or cramps.

- He has burns around his mouth or lips.

- He has a strong, unfamiliar breath odor.

If any of these signs are present, or even if none of them is but you *suspect* your child might have poisoned himself, the first thing you must do is call your local Poison Control Center (the number should be posted next to the phone) and follow their instructions!

Even if you are not completely sure that what your child took *is* poisonous, call the Poison Control Center. They will tell you what to do immediately and will talk you through any poison emergency. Also remember the following:

- Have the container of whatever the child swallowed when you call so you can give the Poison Control Center any information they need about what your child took. Do not follow instructions on the label as they may be incorrect.

- If your child vomits, save a sample of what he has thrown up. You may have to take it to the emergency room.

- Keep freshly dated *syrup of ipecac* in the house. It will make your child vomit—but *do not* use it unless you are told to do so by the Poison Control Center.

- Never induce vomiting if your child has swallowed a corrosive or a petroleum product (something that burns—acid or alkali). *Corrosives* include strong detergents, oven cleansers, drain openers, and dishwasher detergents. *Petroleum products* are things such as furniture polish, bug and insect sprays, and gasoline. Vomiting a corrosive or a petroleum product can cause severe complications.

- If you know your child has swallowed a corrosive, you see the container, or he is complaining that his mouth, lips, or tongue burn, give him milk or water to sip slowly if he is fully conscious and alert. He should sip slowly so he won't vomit. Don't give him anything to drink if he has swallowed a petroleum product, unless instructed to do so by the Poison Control Center.

Inhaled Poisons: Carbon monoxide is the most commonly inhaled poison.

It is present not only in car exhausts but in lanterns, charcoal grills, and gas used for cooking and heating. Carbon monoxide is completely odorless and tasteless, and a child can die within a few minutes of inhaling it.

The signs and symptoms of carbon monoxide poisoning are headache and dizziness, yawning, lethargy, and nausea or vomiting.

The most immediate thing you must do if you think your child has inhaled carbon monoxide or any other toxic fumes is to get him out in the *fresh air*, take care of the *AIRWAY, BREATHING, CIRCULATION*, and get medical help immediately!

HEAD INJURIES

Approximately a quarter of a million children are hospitalized every year with serious head injuries. Little babies, especially, are top heavy, and when they fall, they often hit their heads first!

The very first thing you must do with any serious head injury is check to see if your child is conscious. If he is unconscious, remember to open his *AIRWAY*, check his *BREATHING* and his *CIRCULATION*. Important things to keep in mind when giving first aid are:

- Be especially careful moving the child, since *there is always the possibility of a neck or spine injury with any serious head injury.*

- Stop any bleeding by placing a sterile dressing on the wound. (Don't press too hard because the skull may be fractured.)

- Don't try to clean an open head wound. Get emergency help immediately!

Even after a seemingly minor bump or bruise on the head, *watch your child closely for at least twenty-four hours.* Look for anything out of the ordinary that starts right after the injury or shortly thereafter. A head injury that doesn't appear serious at first could become serious because of slow bleeding or swelling inside the head. This is why you should always talk to your pediatrician right after any head injury. The following signs are considered serious, and you should get medical help immediately:

- Any loss of consciousness, *no matter how brief.*

- Momentary bewilderment. If your child cries immediately after hitting his head, that's probably a good sign. If he seems momentarily dazed or bewildered, he might have a concussion.

- Seizures.

- A large swelling, or any increase in swelling at the injury site.

- Bleeding or fluid coming from the nose or ears.

- Unusual black-and-blue marks, or bruises behind the ears or under the eyes. (This could indicate internal bleeding.)

• Persistent vomiting or nausea.

• Prolonged crying in an infant.

• Headache, dizziness, or double vision.

• Dramatic change in behavior: Your child suddenly becomes quiet or inactive, or unusually lethargic or sleepy, or he becomes very irritable and agitated. (BABY-LIFE parents are told always to consider any change in behavior a serious sign after a head injury, an accident, or during an illness.)

• Pupils of unequal size, or pupils that don't constrict when a light is shined into them. (A small percentage of babies are actually born with unequal-size pupils. You should check this on your child.)

While most bumps to your child's head probably will not be serious, remember, *anything at all that looks unusual*, even after a minor head injury, should be reported to your pediatrician immediately!

FEBRILE CONVULSIONS

Febrile convulsions are not uncommon in infants and young children up to about age six. Although they are rarely life-threatening, they can be a frightening enough experience to panic any parent!

A febrile convulsion can happen when a child develops a high fever or has a fever that spikes suddenly. Febrile convulsions are usually over almost as quickly as they start, and there is no way to stop a convulsion while a child is having it.

Even though febrile convulsions are less serious than epileptic or other kinds of seizures, the symptoms of any convulsion are often the same:

- You may notice a faraway or "out of it" look to your child, and his eyes may roll.

- His body may suddenly become rigid and stiff.

- He may foam at the mouth and drool excessively.

- His lips may turn blue.

- There may be jerking movements or violent, uncontrolled thrashing of his head and limbs.

- After the convulsion, your child may go into a deep sleep.

Never try to restrain your child, but protect him while he is having a convulsion:

- Cradle your child and protect him from injuring himself, especially his head.

- Keep him on his side, in case of vomiting, and to keep his tongue from blocking his airway.

- Never put your child in a tub of water while he is having a convulsion.

- Never put anything in his mouth and never give a child who is not fully conscious and alert anything to eat or drink.

Get medical help or advice immediately! To help your doctor determine whether your child has suffered a febrile convulsion or something far more serious, note how long the seizure lasted, and exactly what kind of movements your child made.

BROKEN BONES

Children often fall and break bones. This happens more frequently with young children than with infants and babies, whose bones are softer.

If your child breaks a bone, there will almost always be pain, tenderness, swelling, and discoloration. The child will probably guard his injured limb and won't be able to move it. You might also see obvious deformity.

Fractures: There are basically two kinds of fractures: An *open fracture,* where you will see bleeding and you may even see exposed bone ends, and a *closed fracture,* where the skin is not broken. (In a closed fracture, however, you might see superficial skin lacerations.) Young children often get a "greenstick" fracture, which is an incomplete break, because their bones are more elastic.

Fractures, particularly in children, must be confirmed by an X-ray. So, even if you only suspect that your child has a broken bone, and if he is showing *any* of the signs, treat it as if it were a fracture. *Keep the injured part immobilized* and get emergency medical assistance immediately.

Young bones knit quickly, but they must be set properly or there can be lifelong consequences! Mishandling or moving a fractured limb improperly can cause damage to nerves and to the bone ends, or can turn a closed fracture into an open fracture:

• Never try to pull a limb back into place or to force it in any way.

• Keep the limb in the most comfortable position.

• Support it and keep it from moving.

• Use cold compresses for pain, if necessary.

• If bone ends are protruding, *don't try to push the bones back in!* Stop the bleeding and keep the wound covered with a sterile compress.

Dislocations: Dislocations of the shoulder and the elbow often occur in babies and in young children when they are pulled or yanked by the arm. The signs of dislocation are pain, tenderness, deformity, and swelling *at the joint.* Treat a dislocation as you would a fracture. Support it, keep it from moving, and get medical assistance.

Note: If your child is in pain after a fall, check his entire body for swelling or tenderness. Very often a young child falls and uses his hands to stop the fall, and the impact can break his collarbone.

BITES AND STINGS

Insect Bites and Stings: It is probably inevitable that your child will suffer minor insect bites and stings. Mosquitoes, for instance, seem to be attracted to babies and young children more often than to adults.

For minor insect bites and stings, apply cold compresses. Other remedies that will help soothe the itching and pain are calamine lotion or a paste of baking soda and water.

If your child gets a *bee sting* and the stinger remains in the skin, remove it as carefully as you can, trying not to squeeze the stinger as this may get more venom into the skin.

The best way to remove a *tick* from your child's skin is with a tweezers. After stretching the skin taut, pull out the tick *parallel to the skin*, making sure that all parts have been removed. Tug gently and be patient. *Be careful to make sure all of the tick is removed.* Gently wash the site of the tick bite with soap and water, and use an antiseptic. If you are unable to remove the tick completely, get medical attention.

Caution: Always call your pediatrician after a tick bite, especially if anything unusual develops, such as a rash, redness, swelling, a fever, muscle aches, or headaches. Ticks carry Rocky Mountain spotted fever, Colorado tick fever, and Lyme disease.

Human or Animal Bites: The treatment for a human or animal bite is similar to the treatment for any other wound that breaks the skin. If your child gets a human or animal bite:

- Stop any bleeding with direct pressure.

- Gently wash the wound with soap and warm water, and flush thoroughly with water.

- Pat dry and apply a sterile gauze dressing.

- Always call your pediatrician immediately, because the biggest danger from bites, especially human bites, is the possibility of infection. With animal bites, there is a remote possibility of rabies.

Snakebites: Since you may not always be sure whether the snake that bites your child is poisonous, it is vital that you get medical advice as quickly as possible after any snakebite!

There are only two types of poisonous snake in the United States—the coral snake and the pit vipers, which include rattlesnakes, copperheads, and water moccasins.

All poisonous snakes, with the exception of the coral snake, have fangs and vertical pupils. The coral snake has teeth and horizonal pupils, and is identified by colorful bands of red, yellow, and black that touch each other. The signs and symptoms of *coral snake* bite are:

- Possibly little or no pain where bitten

- Gradually increasing drowsiness

- Slurred speech

- Blurred vision

- Droopy eyelids

- Increased salivation and sweating

Some of the signs and symptoms you might see after a bite by a *pit viper*:

- One or more fang marks

- Possible extreme pain at the site of the wound

- Swelling and discoloration

- Weakness and shortness of breath

- Nausea and vomiting

If you think your child has been bitten by a poisonous snake, you will have to *act immediately*, since even a small amount of venom can affect a young child more severely than it would an adult!

The first thing you must do is *call your local* Poison Control Center *and follow their instructions!* Then have your child lie down and *keep him as still as possible.* Continually reassure your child and *keep him calm* while you are giving him first aid. This is extremely important, since the venom will spread through his body more quickly if he becomes anxious and agitated:

- If your child is bitten on the arm or leg, keep the limb at heart level and immobilized.

- Wash the bite with soap and water, being careful not to move or agitate the limb unnecessarily as this will make the venom spread more quickly.

• Never apply ice or cold water to a snakebite.

If you can't reach the Poison Control Center, get your child to a hospital as quickly as possible!

Caution: Both the use of constricting bands and suctioning the venom are controversial and can cause more damage if done improperly! They should only be attempted by someone who is medically qualified. You must make every effort to get your child to a doctor or a medical facility as soon as he is bitten by a poisonous snake.

Spiders and Scorpions: Insects

such as spiders and scorpions can also give your child poisonous bites. The black widow and brown recluse are the two poisonous spiders found in the United States.

You may not necessarily know the kind of spider that bites your child, so if you even *think* your child has been bitten by *any* spider, *call* Poison Control *immediately*, or get him to a doctor or hospital as soon as possible!

Some of the signs and symptoms you might see after a *black widow* spider bite are:

• A sharp pain that later subsides.

• Severe cramps in the stomach, thighs, or back, about half an hour to two hours after the bite.

• Breathing difficulties, tremors, and pain in the legs and the arms.

The bite of a *brown recluse* spider might go unnoticed, but a severe skin reaction could develop later, along with chills and fever.

ALLERGIC REACTIONS

Children can have a serious allergic reaction to foods, medication such as penicillin, or the bite or sting of an insect, especially bees, wasps, hornets, and yellow jackets. This can cause *anaphylactic shock*, and life-threatening symptoms can develop within moments. Some of these signs and symptoms might be:

• Breathing difficulties or wheezing

• Itching and burning of the skin

• Redness of the face, neck, and chest

• Hives

• Swelling of the eyes, face, or tongue

• Appearance of an extensive rash

• Restlessness and anxiety

• Nausea and vomiting

Sometimes the only sign will be a sudden loss of consciousness. If your child does become unconscious, *remember to take care of the AIRWAY, BREATHING, and CIRCULATION first!*

The usual treatment for anaphylactic shock is administering epinephrine by injection. This is why it is *urgent* that you get medical help as soon as possible if your child has *any* signs or symptoms of anaphylactic shock. *Minutes count!*

Caution: Even if your child doesn't show any dramatic signs of an allergic attack, but seems to be having any kind of generalized allergic reaction, get medical advice immediately.

HEATSTROKE

Heatstroke occurs when a child is extremely overheated and his body-temperature regulating mechanism has broken down. It is truly a life-threatening emergency, and young children are very susceptible to it.

For instance, if you leave your baby or young child alone in a car on a hot day, even with the window slightly open, your child could suffer heat-stroke. (Children have actually died this way!)

If your child develops heatstroke, his temperature could soar to 104 degrees F., or even higher. Other signs you will notice are:

- He might not sweat, even though he is very hot. (This is one of the most typical signs of heatstroke.)

- His skin will become flushed, hot, and dry.

- He will become disoriented and confused. He may possibly even go into a coma.

The first thing you must do if you think your child is suffering from heatstroke is get emergency medical assistance and *cool your child off immediately:*

- Place your child in a tub of cold water or under a cold shower. (Never use ice or icy water.) Use a garden hose to cool him down if you are unable to put him in the tub or under a shower.

- You can wrap him in cold wet towels or sheets, or sponge him with cold water.

- Be sure to cool his head.

- You can use an air conditioner or fan to help cool him off. (If you don't have these appliances, put him in the coolest room of the house.)

- Cool your child quickly, but *be careful not to overcool or chill him!* When his temperature drops to 102 degrees F., stop cooling, but keep watching him and make sure his temperature continues to drop naturally. If it starts to rise again, resume your cooling efforts. Remember to get emergency medical help as soon as possible!

HEAT EXHAUSTION

HYPOTHERMIA

Heat exhaustion differs from heat-stroke in that your child's body temperature will remain normal, or slightly below normal. (His body-temperature regulating mechanism is still functioning.) He will perspire, and his skin will feel clammy. He will also feel weak, have a headache, be nauseated or vomit, and feel faint.

Heat exhaustion is usually caused by overexertion in hot weather. If your child suffers from heat exhaustion, take him out of the sun. Take him inside or to a shaded area. Give him something to sip if he is conscious and alert—a commercially prepared electrolyte-replacement drink (get your pediatrician to recommend one to keep on hand) juice, lemonade, or water with a sprinkling of salt in it. (If he vomits, stop the fluids and get emergency medical help!)

Have your child lie down, elevate his feet, loosen his clothing, and apply cold compresses and fan him. You can also put him in an air-conditioned room. *Call your pediatrician immediately.*

Hypothermia can occur when your child is overexposed to the cold and his internal body temperature drops.

Children lose body heat more quickly than adults, so hypothermia is something that easily occurs in cold weather, especially if your child's clothing becomes damp or wet, or he is exposed to a strong, cold wind.

Hypothermia can come on a child very slowly and almost without notice. Your child may appear only quiet and listless in the early stages, so be especially alert to his behavior in very cold weather. If your child is suffering from hypothermia:

- You might see waves of violent shivering.

- He may become numb.

- His speech may be slurred.

- He might experience muscle weakness or a loss of muscle coordination.

- He may become lethargic.

The first thing you must do if you suspect your child is suffering from hypothermia is to get him indoors immediately! If this is not possible, shelter him from the wind and try to use your own body to help warm him. *What is most important is to protect your child from any further heat loss:*

• Remove all wet clothing

• Wrap him in warm blankets or a sleeping bag. (Make sure he is well insulated from the ground.)

• Cover his head to prevent further heat loss.

• Using your own body heat through close physical contact is a very effective way to help warm him. (Skin-to-skin contact is best.)

• Give him warm liquids to drink *if* he is fully conscious and alert.

• Use any kind of external heat that is at hand—such as hot-water bottles, electric blankets, a heater, or a campfire. Make sure that the external heat source is well insulated or far enough away from your child so that it does not accidently burn him.

• *Get medical assistance immedi-*

ately, even if your child seems to have recovered. *In children, all causes of hypothermia should be considered serious!*

Caution: In severe cases of hypothermia, your child's body must be rewarmed *slowly* to avoid a shock to his system. Get emergency medical help immediately, and *be especially gentle and careful while you are handling your child.*

FROSTBITE

Infants and young children are more susceptible to frostbite than adults. Frostbite can happen subtly; the signs and symptoms are not always obvious. This is why it is so important to watch your baby or young child when he is out in extremely cold weather.

Most often, frostbite affects the nose, ears, fingers, toes, and cheeks:

- His skin will feel extremely cold and may become slightly flushed before the onset of frostbite.

- His skin will lose color at first, but as the frostbite becomes more advanced it may appear glossy white or grayish yellow, or white and mottled.

- Blisters may develop.

- There may be pain, or your child *may not even realize* he has been frostbitten.

If your child shows signs of frostbite:

- Cover or warm the frostbitten area with other body parts. (For instance, tucking fingers under arms.)

- Get your child indoors.

- Rewarm the frozen part by putting it in warm, *not hot*, water. (Test the water with your inner arm. It should not feel hot.) *Rewarm only until the frostbitten part becomes flushed pink.* If warm water is not available, use warm blankets or clothing to wrap the frostbitten area lightly.

- Give your child something warm to drink.

- Keep frostbitten fingers and toes separated with cloth or gauze, if possible.

- Never rub the frostbitten area.

- Never apply direct heat to frostbite.

- Don't allow the thawed part to become refrozen!

- Get medical assistance as quickly as possible!

DEHYDRATION

Just as a small loss of blood can be dangerous to a baby or young child, any loss of fluid can be equally threatening!

That's why persistent diarrhea or vomiting should be considered serious, and you should talk to your pediatrician immediately! (Even overexposure to the sun can cause a baby to become dehydrated.)

Keep a commercially prepared electrolyte-replacement drink on hand (your pediatrician can recommend one), so that even if you can't reach your pediatrician right away, you can begin giving it to your baby to maintain his electrolyte balance. (Electrolyte minerals such as potassium and sodium are vital to life, and in small babies these are quickly lost from vomiting or diarrhea.)

FOREIGN OBJECTS IN THE EARS AND NOSE

Never probe in your child's ears or nose, and never remove any foreign object from your child's ears or nose unless you can see it and reach it easily! Call your pediatrician or get medical assistance.

If you are removing something from your child's nose, make sure he is sitting up so you will not push it farther back into his nose. When removing something from his ear, *be careful not to push it farther in*. It can damage his eardrum. Sometimes an object in an ear will dislodge more easily if your child tilts his head to the side.

Part VII
Important Safety Tips

IMPORTANT SAFETY TIPS

Parents in BABY-LIFE classes often ask when to start baby-proofing their homes: You must start creating a safe environment from the moment your baby comes home! Even before your baby is born, you should become aware of the safety hazards in your home!

Constant supervision is the key to keeping your baby safe. Even when he is sleeping in his crib, the baby should be within easy hearing distance.

When you are busy, or even when you are only momentarily distracted by the phone or the doorbell, take the baby with you or put him in a crib or playpen.

Be extra careful when visiting friends or relatives whose homes are not child-safe.

Never leave a child alone in the house!

Never let children walk around with pencils, scissors, forks, or other sharp objects.

Children are more likely to have accidents when they are hungry and tired, before a meal or before bedtime.

Never shake an infant or toss him up in the air! Neck and spinal injuries— even brain damage and death—can result!

Keep knives and other sharp utensils away from the edges of countertops and tables. Make sure knives are stored up high, out of baby's reach, or in locked drawers children cannot open.

The trash can could be the most dangerous playground in the house. Tin-can lids can slice small fingers, broken glass can cut them, and discarded plastic bags can suffocate a baby. Keep trash where your child cannot possibly get into it!

Never, ever leave a child alone in a car—not even for a moment. Remember, on hot days the interior of a car can become so hot that your child will suffer heatstroke. Children have actually died this way!

Never give your child an ice cube to suck on. Children choke on them!

Be very careful around car doors. Also, watch your child's fingers near doorways, and keep them away from the backs of doors (especially in stores and supermarkets). It is possible for a young child to lose part of a finger by getting it caught in a closing door.

Keep very young children, especially infants, out of direct sunlight during the peak hours of 10 A.M. to 2 P.M. Even during off-peak hours, make sure children are protected from direct exposure to the sun. Use a sun block if that is recommended by your pediatrician.

Be extra careful in cars with electric windows. Children have died when their necks have become entrapped in automatic windows.

The accident rate for children goes up on weekends and when there is a new care-giver—so be especially vigilant then.

Babies learn new things every day— even from one moment to the next!

Never underestimate your child's abilities. What he can't do today he'll be able to do tomorrow. Remember, constant supervision is the key to keeping your child safe.

Never leave appliance or electrical cords dangling over the edge of countertops. Remember that babies love to reach up and pull down!

One of the best ways to child-proof your home is to take a safety crawl. Get down on your hands and knees and crawl around wherever your baby crawls. You'll notice things such as the little rubber ends on doorstops that your baby could put in his mouth and choke on. You'll also find what is really on your floor—coins lost under furniture, a missing earring, paper clips. When you look at your home from a child's perspective, you will suddenly discover all kinds of dangers you didn't realize existed!

Never prop a bottle for an infant. If he starts to inhale the liquid and cannot push it away, he could choke.

Never leave a baby or young child alone while he is eating!

Tell older children in the family not to give food to the baby! Many babies have actually choked to death after older siblings gave them inappropriate food, such as pieces of a hot dog. Also, keep older children's toys such as marbles, hobby sets, small wooden or rubber balls, and jack sets away from young babies!

If you have children's furniture or equipment that is made of metal tubing, such as high chairs, playpens, or infant seats, check to be sure that the plugs or caps on the ends of the tubing cannot be pulled off. They can easily choke a child.

Pencils with removable decorative erasers and ornaments are a frightening new choking hazard for children. The eraser can easily come off in the child's mouth and become lodged in the throat.

Infants sleeping in parents' beds have actually been suffocated by dozing parents rolling over on them.

Children can become entrapped and suffocate in any airtight container. Remove the doors from discarded refrigerators and freezers immediately.

Lead-based paint is often found on old or repainted furniture, windowsills, railings, or outdoor furniture. Don't let children chew on such things.

Each year many young children kill themselves, and their siblings and friends, with firearms! Guns must be stored unloaded, out of sight and out of reach, in a locked cabinet that a child has absolutely no access to. Store ammunition separately!

Never give your baby frozen bagels, carrots, crackers, or any food to teethe on. A piece of the food can break off and choke the baby.

Don't give babies paper to play with. They can easily choke on it.

Giving a baby a bottle in a moving car can be very dangerous if the car hits a bump. The baby could aspirate or inhale the liquid.

Never leave a baby alone in the middle of a bed, and never, ever take your hand off a baby on a changing table.

Babies and young children frequently pull off Band-Aids and put them in their mouths. This can be dangerous!

SETTING LIMITS

As your child gets older, you must continue to keep his environment safe, but you must also begin to set limits and point out dangers to your child: Where he may go and where he may not go; what he can and cannot play with. Part of setting limits is teaching your child to understand what is *safe* and what is *dangerous*. Use gestures and your voice to show him the difference.

Even a young baby will understand "No!" and "Dangerous!" if these words are spoken in a gruff, harsh manner. A pleasant voice can be used to show him what is safe. Be persistent in teaching your child the difference between safe and dangerous, and he will gradually learn to protect himself.

Don't be *too* trusting, however! Your child may or may not completely understand the difference between safe and dangerous, so you must still depend on constant supervision and continually create a safe environment!

BABY-LIFE
Emergency Information

Mother's Name

Father's Name

Home Address

Telephone Number

Child's Name

Date of Birth

Allergies

Medicines Taken Regularly

Blood Type

Other Medical Information

Child's Name

Date of Birth

Allergies

Medicines Taken Regularly

Blood Type

Other Medical Information